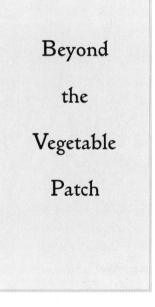

GARDENS

Beyond

the

Vegetable

Patch

▚

Carole Turner-Guest Editor

FOR THE
ADVANCE
MENT OF
BOTANY
AND THE
SERVICE OF
THE CITY

BROOKLYN
BOTANIC
GARDEN
PUBLICATIONS
· MCMXCVIII ·

Janet Marinelli
SERIES EDITOR

Beth Hanson
MANAGING EDITOR

Bekka Lindstrom
ART DIRECTOR

Stephen K-M. Tim
VICE PRESIDENT, SCIENCE, LIBRARY & PUBLICATIONS

Judith D. Zuk
PRESIDENT

Elizabeth Scholtz
DIRECTOR EMERITUS

Handbook #154

Copyright © Spring 1998 by the Brooklyn Botanic Garden, Inc.

Handbooks in the 21st-Century Gardening Series, formerly Plants & Gardens,
are published quarterly at 1000 Washington Ave., Brooklyn, NY 11225.

Subscription included in Brooklyn Botanic Garden subscriber membership dues ($35.00 per year).

ISSN # 0362-5850 ISBN # 1-889538-05-1

Printed by Science Press, a division of the Mack Printing Group

Table of Contents

THE KITCHEN GARDEN

Beyond the Vegetable Patch

BY CAROLE TURNER

SIMPLY PUT, a kitchen garden is a place to grow things that you bring into the kitchen—vegetables, fruits and berries, herbs, edible flowers and cut flowers. It is a place of beauty and bounty, a place that stimulates and delights all the senses. The perfect blend of aesthetics and utility, the kitchen garden is a paradise where you can not just look, touch, and smell, but also taste.

The kitchen garden is a place of activity, season after season: something's always sprouting, blooming, being harvested—being tasted.

No mere vegetable garden, a kitchen garden has style, reflecting your personal taste and the flavor of your particular region of the country.

No matter how simple or small, a kitchen garden makes its owner feel like the lord or lady of the manor. My own garden is only 20 feet square, but when I open the gate and go in, I always swell with pride as I stroll up and down the aisles surveying the fruits of my labor (and popping a few in my mouth).

No mere vegetable garden, a kitchen garden has style. Even if you don't grow gourmet or "designer" vegetables, or antique fruits or flowers, or chic varieties of herbs, the kitchen garden can reflect your personal taste and the flavor of your particular region of the country. There are no rules: The kitchen garden can look like a perennial border, or an English cottage garden, or even an Oriental garden. It can have a Southwestern desert look, complete with edible cacti, or it can be romantic, strewn with roses and smelling of lavender and thyme.

If you're of an orderly bent, you can plant your kitchen garden in traditional rows, with sturdy bamboo tepees and trellises for climbing vegetables. Or you can take a more casual approach, making a garden that is a tumble of flowers interspersed with greens, colorful peppers, eggplants, squash blossoms, and cooking herbs. There are so many attractive ways to use vegetables and herbs that the modern kitchen garden invites creativity. Edge a flower bed with curly parsley, or pair your tomato plants with pot marigolds, or grow fluffy green clumps of lettuce around the bases of red cabbages.

Whatever you choose to do, don't leave any bare spots. Every space should be used, every inch devoted to food and flowers. And when one thing is harvested, put another in. The kitchen garden is a place of activity, season after season. There should always be something growing, something being harvested, something blooming, something sprouting. The rewards will be many, and not all tangible. The kitchen garden, after all, is a place to feed both body and soul.

Kitchen gardens have evolved out of regional farming and culinary traditions that stretch back hundreds of years. In England, the cottage garden style originated in the Middle Ages as one of the many repercussions of the black plague; English kitchen gardens are still often planted in that Medieval style. In France, kitchen gardens evolved from the very geometric, stylized gardens of France's past into today's loose, romantic, and lush **potagers.** North America has its own kitchen garden traditions, which borrow from the styles familiar to immigrants to the New World. In the following section, you'll find tips on designing a kitchen garden that works for you.

A TRADITIONAL AMERICAN KITCHEN GARDEN

Thomas Jefferson's Monticello

BY PETER J. HATCH

I have often thought that if heaven had given me choice of my position and calling, it would have been on a rich spot of earth, well watered, and near a good market for the productions of the garden. No occupation is so delightful to me as the culture of the earth, and no culture comparable to that of the garden. Such a variety of subjects, some one always coming to perfection, the failure of one thing repaired by the success of another, and instead of one harvest a continued one through the year. Under a total want of demand except for our family table, I am still devoted to the garden. But though an old man, I am but a young gardener.

—Thomas Jefferson to
Charles Willson Peale, 1811

WHEN THOMAS JEFFERSON referred to his "garden," he, like most early Americans, was reserving the term for his vegetable garden, a 1,000-foot-long terrace on the southeastern side of his "little mountain" in Charlottesville, Virginia. Jefferson's garden not only supplied the family table, but also served as a kind of laboratory where he experimented with

70 different species of vegetables. Jefferson grew as many as 40 types of bean and 17 lettuce varieties, then selectively eliminated inferior sorts through the scientific method: "I am curious to select one or two of the best species or variety of every garden vegetable, and to reject all others from the garden to avoid the dangers of mixing or degeneracy."

Jefferson's garden evolved over many years. In 1770 he began by growing crops along the contours of the slope, then introduced terracing in 1806, and by 1812, gardening activity was at its peak. One visitor described the terrace or garden plateau, which was literally hewed from the side of the mountain, as a "hanging garden."

The heart of the two-acre garden, which is still cultivated today, is divided into 24 "squares," or growing plots. According to an 1812 account, the squares were arranged according to which part of the plant was being harvested—whether "fruits" (tomatoes, beans), "roots" (beets), or "leaves" (lettuce, cabbage). Jefferson planted tomatoes, cucumbers, and peas in the garden's northwest border very early in the season. The grassy bank beside this border radiated warmth, probably giving him a decided advantage in the annual spring pea contests. The site and situation of the garden enabled Jefferson to grow tender vegetables into the winter months. Because cold air settles in low areas, on this small mountaintop, late spring frosts are unusual and the first freezing temperatures in early fall rarely occur before Thanksgiving.

Jefferson added some ornamental features to the terrace garden, and wrote about planting different flowering shades of "arbor" bean ("purple, red, scarlet, and white"). He also arranged adjacent rows of purple-, white-, and green-sprouting broccoli, or even white and purple eggplant, and he bordered his tomato square with sesame or okra, a rather unusual juxtaposition of plant textures.

Along with English peas, figs, artichokes, tomatoes, eggplants, broccoli, and cauliflowers, Jefferson cherished asparagus.

Jefferson's garden evolved over many years, but the heart of the two-acre garden was the 24 "squares," or growing plots, that are still cultivated today.

Salads were an important part of Jefferson's diet. He would note the planting of lettuce and radishes every two weeks through the growing season. He grew interesting greens like orach, corn salad, endive, and nasturtium, and planted sesame so that he could make a suitable salad oil. While the English pea is believed to have been his favorite vegetable, he also cherished figs, asparagus, artichokes, and such "new" vegetables as tomatoes, eggplants, broccoli, and cauliflowers. Jefferson cultivated common crops like cucumbers, cabbages, and beans (both "snaps" for fresh use and "haricots" that were dried), and also prized unusual ones such as sea kale (*Crambe maritima*), a perennial cabbage-like species whose spring sprouts were blanched in pots, then cut and prepared like asparagus.

Many of the varieties originally grown by Jefferson are now impossible to find or even identify, since he often named them according to the person from whom he received the seed ("Leitch's pea"), its place of origin ("Tuscan bean"), a physical characteristic such as color ("yellow carrot"), or season of harvest ("forward pea"). In many cases, the varieties now grown in the garden were known in the 19th century but not necessarily those planted by Jefferson. Today, the garden serves as an important preservation seed bank of 19th-century vegetable varieties—and provides Monticello employees with bumper crops of vegetables harvested from Jefferson's garden.

THE FOUR-SQUARE

A Classic Kitchen Garden Design

BY JOHN D. SIMPSON

IKE A COUNTRY KITCHEN, a four-square kitchen garden evokes thoughts of hearth, home, and abundance. It is a garden design based on a very simple layout that provides a rich, unpretentious display of color, form, and, quite literally, good taste. Refined through the centuries, the four-square has been an integral part of home life and, like a good kitchen, is a place where you can have beauty and eat it, too.

The history of the classic four-square garden goes back seven centuries, to the first English cottage gardens. The English cottage garden style was born not of abundance but in a society crippled by the Black Death of the 12th century. The plague so decimated the working peasantry that, to garner a work force for the landholding aristocracy, landlords offered land and cottages in exchange for crops. The gardens that sprouted up around these cottages became a hallmark of English culture for hundreds of years. They were planted in the traditional four-square layout.

Early cottage gardens were commonly divided into four rectangular plots by two intersecting paths—hence the term "four-square." This arrangement made it easier to cultivate crops such as grains, vegetables, herbs, berries, and fruits, and sometimes even to raise livestock. Flowers ultimately found their way into the gardens, becoming an essential part of the cottage garden style. Today's four-square gardens, typically smaller than their predecessors, may devote as much space to flowers as to salads. There is plenty of room for originality, so no two gardens need ever be alike.

The four-square kitchen garden is based on a very simple layout that allows plenty of room for originality, rich color and form, and, quite literally, good taste.

Make space in your garden for entertaining. Leave all or part of one of the squares open for an outdoor terrace where you can sit and watch your plants grow.

Designing a four-square garden

A traditional English four-square garden is usually situated in the front yard, but modern yard arrangements make it both practical and appropriate to put the kitchen garden in the backyard. No matter where the garden is located, it should include four elements: an enclosure, an entry gateway, a T-shaped path system to delineate the planting beds, and a rich mixture of plantings.

Enclosure To create a design for your garden, picture it as an outdoor room that first needs a good set of walls. A protective enclosure such as a masonry wall, fence, hedge, or closely planted trees creates this necessary boundary; the more solid the barrier, the more secure and cozy the interior of the garden will feel. Dry-laid stone walls usually make the most elegant enclosures, while wood fences are less labor intensive. A hedge is a reasonably priced alternative, but it may take time to grow to a mature size. One way to create additional interest is to vary your materials—you might build a brick wall for one side of the enclosure, and a hedge for another, for instance. Consider both aesthetics and surrounding structures when making your choices.

Entry gateway A gate not only gives the garden some form of entry, but it also helps to provide a signature style by hinting at the garden's mood within.

Depending on the design and materials used, the gateway can suggest formality, informality, whimsy, even humor. Historically, simple white picket gates provided entry to a cottage garden. Today, arbors and trellises draped in flowering vines are popular and reinforce the message that this is a special place.

Path system The traditional four-square layout is created by straight paths, one leading from the garden gate to the front entry of the house, and the other crossing it at a 90-degree angle. Absolute symmetry is not a requirement, so pathways can be offset to accommodate gates and doors. Depending on available space, the intersection of the two paths can also become a natural focal point. If you have enough room, consider carving out a circular area in which to place a sculpture, cistern, or other ornament.

The paths can be made of just about any material, from wood shavings to brick to stone to lawn. This flexible palette makes it possible to start conservatively—say, with gravel or compacted earth—and plan for future indulgences of stone or brick. Use materials that are appropriate for your region.

Plants for the four-square garden

Plants soften the linear austerity of a four-square garden. Think in terms of abundance, starting with the border plants. Beds can be edged in shrubs, annuals, or perennials, depending on the size of the garden. If you have room for a hedge, choose a pleasing color and leaf texture since the hedge will be a backdrop for the other plants. Clipped English boxwoods (*Buxus sempervirens*) provide a traditional evergreen look. Other shrubs for hedges include photinia (*Photinia fraseri*), yews (*Taxus* species), hornbeams (*Carpinus* species), or some combination of these. Roses and pruned trees can also act as hedges in large gardens. For a more colorful look or a smaller garden, use low-growing flowers such as dwarf irises, daffodils, tulips, or lush lavenders to edge your beds.

Vegetables are the stars of the kitchen garden, and you can combine various vegetable colors and textures for innumerable design possibilities—plant kale in a diamond pattern and surround it with onions or radishes, for instance. Outside of the basic four-square structure, there are really no rules to this type of garden.

Use herbs for edging, as fillers, or as accent plants. Plant creeping thyme along walkways, where it can spill out underfoot and release wonderful fragrance when stepped upon. Shrubby herbs like rosemary or sage create low, continuous borders if they are kept neatly trimmed.

Fruit trees are also essential for a complete kitchen garden. Of all the plants in the kitchen garden, they embrace the broadest range of seasons with displays of flowers, fruits, leaf color, and branch patterns. Plant fruit trees "orchard style" in one square, form a boundary planting, or even tumble them over a wall. Don't plant fruit trees throughout the garden, though, unless you can live with the resulting shade. If space is at a premium, espalier trees against a wall or a trellis or find dwarf varieties.

Vines are another feature in traditional four-square gardens. They give a garden a lived-in look, softening architecture and taking floral color to new heights. They are at their best twining around entryway arbors and gateposts, or clinging to walls and fences. Some good choices are Virginia creeper (*Parthenocissus quinquefolia*) and vine honeysuckles (*Lonicera* species)—but avoid Japanese honeysuckle *(L. japonica),* which is invasive. For color and edible fruit, choose from a wide variety of grapes, based on your climate. For color and fragrance, try wisteria (*Wisteria floribunda*) or climbing roses. Sweet peas and morning glories are fast-growing annual vines that can provide flowers quickly.

Finally, what is a kitchen without fresh cut flowers? Every kitchen garden must have them. Plant a corner of sunflowers to rise above the crowd, or tulips in a line to highlight a spring planting of lettuce. Or put a large planter in the center of the garden, and fill it with daffodils, cosmos, cornflowers, or whatever your heart desires. In a four-square garden, nearly anything goes.

Modern touches

If your house is contemporary, a traditional English-style cottage garden may not be appropriate, but it doesn't take much to give a four-square garden a modern look. Sculpture, for instance, can be very dramatic within the simple lines of the four-square. If the garden is large, try placing sculptural pieces in "hideaway" locations where they can be discovered. Be careful not to dominate the setting with overly large pieces, or you will destroy the inherent simplicity of the garden. Likewise, avoid curving pathways unless the garden is situated on a slope; there is a point at which the simple charm of the four-square can be lost to too many curves.

Since we tend to use our outdoor areas for entertainment more often than the 12th-century English peasants did, we should make space in the garden for this purpose. Leave all or part of one of the squares open for an outdoor terrace so you can enjoy the fruits of your labor while you watch them grow. The "floor" of this terrace can be anything from turf to gravel to stone pavers to brick. Or for a very contemporary feel, build a wood deck.

Modern four-squares are also tailored to their climates and regions, which can

Vines give a garden a lived-in look, softening architecture and taking floral color to new heights. Twine them around entryway arbors and gateposts, or up walls.

be both a challenge and a great opportunity. Use plants that reflect the regional color palette of plants, sky, and geology. Native dryland plants make a much more natural, appropriate kitchen garden in a desert climate than traditional cottage-garden plants. No matter where you live, a four-square kitchen garden will reward you with seasonal color, edibles, and an outdoor space that will feel like home. ▨

❖

THE *POTAGER*

A Kitchen Garden
in the
French Country Style

BY LOUISA JONES

IN THE FRENCH KITCHEN GARDEN or *potager,* gardeners have intermingled vegetables, fruits, flowers, and herbs since medieval times. For the French, the *potager* has always been the country counterpart of the grand *chateaux parterres. Potagers* are more popular than ever in France; a government survey taken in 1994 revealed that 23 percent of the fruit and vegetables consumed by the French are home-grown.

In France today, *potager* design is typically informal, or romantic. Often called the *jardin de curé,* or country curate's garden, this intimate and sensual style is comparable to that of the English cottage garden, except that it is centered on vegetables rather than flowers. Its inspiration is a complicity with nature rather than a desire to impose order, and this fashion has been fed by the growing influence of organic gardening in France over the last twenty years.

Organic kitchen gardeners are great promoters of biodiversity, and many heirloom vegetable varieties have been saved by their efforts. They also create gardens where local fauna, including birds, insects, and even reptiles feel at home. Their gardens are often called "natural" because of their informal exuberance and spontaneity. The danger is that, as in Emerson's bean patch, respect for all comers means the weeds will eventually smother the vegetables! Each gardener must find his or her own balance with the rest of nature.

Today's *potager* is typically informal, or romantic, with an intimate and sensual style centered on vegetables rather than flowers.

FAST FILLERS FOR THE POTAGER

Alyssum, sweet *(Lobularia maritima)*
Basil *(Ocimum basilicum)*
Chervil *(Anthriscus cereifolium)*
Beans, bush *(Phaseolus vulgaris)*
Cress *(Lepidium sativum)*
Mustard *(Brassica* spp.)
Parsley, curly *(Petroselinum crispum)*
Phacelia *(Phacelia* spp.)
Savory, summer *(Satureja hortensis)*

Planning a potager

Here are some suggestions that will help you create a kitchen garden in the French *potager* style outside your own back door.

• Consider how the site chosen fits into the surrounding landscape. Think about the effects of wind and hours of sunshine, but also consider the overall setting: Will it be a harmonious part of a larger picture, or completely set off by hedges or walls? Vantage point is an important design consideration, so think about where you will see the garden from most often.

• Next, consider the overall design. This will depend primarily on how you plan to cultivate the garden—by hand or by machine (and what kind of machine), which will determine not only the garden's shape but also how wide the paths need to be. Any pattern is possible—spiral, checkerboard, wagon wheel, cubist. As the season progresses and plants grow, the outlines of your beds will evolve. In the informal country style, there is rarely bare earth or much space between rows; the beds are quickly filled in with companion plants, mulch, green manures, or self-sown volunteers.

• A good design includes vertical accents. These can be temporary (a stand of corn, tomato towers, bean tepees, a single angelica plant), or permanent (berry bushes, a small apple cordon). Hedges and walls are also permanent, of course, and can themselves provide food or support for food-bearing plants.

• *Potagers* are essentially tapestries of myriad colors and shapes. The intermingling of herbs, flowers, and fruits with vegetables requires careful placement of perennials so that they do not interfere with the growth of seasonal crops. Small fruit trees traditionally stand at the edge of the *potager*, along paths and walls, with strawberries, annual herbs, or flowers planted at their feet. Aggressive herbs like mint or tansy must be contained. All the annuals mix well with vegetables, and may even serve as beneficial companion plants—for example, planting coriander among carrots, said to deter the carrot fly.

In the past, French kitchen gardens were often composed of parterres, or formally patterned beds like these at the Château de Villandry, near Tours.

PLANTS FOR EDGING BEDS AND PATHS

Basil *(Ocimum basilicum)*

Beans, bush *(Phaseolus vulgaris)*

Bee balm *(Monarda didyma)*

Broccoli *(Brassica oleracea)*

Cabbage, red *(Brassica oleracea)*

Catnip, low-growing *(Nepeta race-mosa* or *N.* x *faassenii* for edging)

Cauliflower *(Brassica oleracea)*

Chives *(Allium schoenoprasum)*

Cosmos *(Cosmos* spp.)

Dahlias, dwarf *(Dahlia* spp.)

Geraniums, fragrant *(Pelargonium* spp.)

Germander *(Teucrium chamaedrys)*

Gladiolus *(Gladiolus* spp.)

Hebe (shrubby veronicas), dwarf *(Hebe* spp.)

Hyssop *(Hyssopus officinalis)*

Irises, dwarf *(Iris* spp.)

Lamb's ears *(Stachys lanata)*

Lavender, dwarf *(Lavandula* spp.)

Lettuce *(Lactuca* spp.)

Mallow *(Lavatera)*, annual varieties

Marigolds, dwarf *(Tagetes* spp.)

Nasturtium, dwarf *(Tropaeolum majus)*—perhaps mixed with beets

Parsley, curly *(Petroselinum crispum)*

Peppers, sweet, hot *(Capsicum* spp.)

Pot marigolds *(Calendula officinalis)*

Rosemary *(Rosmarinus officinalis)*

Rue *(Ruta graveolens)*

Sage *(Salvia officinalis)*

Santolina *(Santolina* spp.)

Savory, summer *(Satureja hortensis)*

Savory, winter *(Satureja montana)*

Sedum *(Sedum spectabile* or *Hylotelephium spectabile)*

Strawberries *(Fragaria* spp.)

Swiss chard *(Betula vulgaris* var. *flavescens*—white-, red-, or yellow-ribbed)

Thyme, bush *(Thymus* spp.)

Violets *(Viola* spp.)

Maintaining the potager year-round

Harvesting vegetables without destroying planting patterns is a challenge in a formal *potager* but less so in the romantic variety, with its more luxuriant growth. Two techniques can help:

• Edge plots with contrasting plants, including herbs and flowers, which will mask bare spots as the season progresses. Choose varieties in keeping with the scale of the garden. Keep free-ranging perennials in bounds with buried strips of metal or plastic.

• After harvesting, use fast fillers such as chervil or cut-and-come-again salad greens. Many of the latter self-sow and can be moved easily to fill gaps when

SELF-SOWERS FOR THE FRENCH KITCHEN GARDEN

Bellflowers, annual *(Campanula* spp.)

Blanket flower *(Gaillardia* spp.)

Chervil *(Anthriscus cereifolium)*

Columbines *(Aquilegia* spp.)

Coreopsis *(Coreopsis* spp.)

Corn cockle (*Agrostemma githago*)

Cosmos *(Cosmos* spp.)

Evening primrose *(Oenothera* spp.)

Fennel *(Foeniculum vulgare)*

Feverfew *(Tanacetum parthenium,* formerly *Chrysanthemum parthenium)*

Fleabane (*Erigeron karvinskianus*)

Gaura *(Gaura lindheimeri)*

Globe thistle *(Echinops ritro)*

Hollyhocks *(Alcea rosea)*

Honesty *(Lunaria annua)*

Larkspur *(Consolida ambigua)*

Lettuces *(Lactuca* spp.)

Love-in-a-mist *(Nigella damascena)*

Mallow *(Lavatera* spp.)

Marigolds *(Tagetes* spp.)

Mullein *(Verbascum* spp.)

Mustard *(Brassica juncea)*

Narcissi *(Narcissus* spp.)

Orach *(Atriplex hortensis)*

Oregano *(Origanum vulgare)*

Phacelia *(Phacelia tanacetifolia)*

Phlomis *(Phlomis* spp.)

Poppy, California (*Eschscholzia californica*)

Spurge, snow-in-summer (*Euphorbia characias*)

Speedwell *(Veronica* spp.)

Sweet peas *(Lathyrus odoratus)*

Toadflax *(Linaria* spp.)

Tobaccos, flowering *(Nicotiana* spp.)

Tulips *(Tulipa* spp.) and other spring bulbs

Valerian, false (*Centranthus ruber*)

Violets *(Viola* spp.)

Wallflower *(Erysimum cheiri)*

required. Fast-growing green manures are ideal: both mustard *(Brassica)* and phacelia *(Phacelia tanacetifolia)* are great favorites in France, both being tough as well as beautiful in flower.

With a bit of effort, your *potager* can be as pleasing as this small Provençal plot described by novelist Henri Bosco, which "nestled under the terrace, sheltered by high, warm walls but open onto the valley full of brown and blue summits, offered to the rosebushes, the tulips, and even to the stray weeds a well of warm air which smelled all at once of fruit trees, hawthorn, and hyssop. Birds twittered among the plums...Nothing was more charming than this garden. It existed in this tiny sheltered bit of land which had trusted itself to man, under the large benevolent house—just big enough for a soul without worldly ambition, or possessing the genius of retirement."

A KITCHEN GARDEN

IN BLOOM

A Combination Cutting and Vegetable Garden

BY SUZY BALES

T WAS WITH FLOWERS that my love of gardening began, so it is only natural that my New York kitchen garden is a mixture of flowers and vegetables. A combination cutting and vegetable garden is not only practical, but also provides the table with flowers for many memorable meals. It encourages imagination and experimentation, and is also immune to criticism, as it is designed first and foremost to be productive. Missteps and clashing colors are not as noticeable as they would be in a flower border; the ubiquitous vegetable greens unite and calm all the colors, no matter how bright. And a garden as colorful and original as a child's crayon drawing is a happy place to work.

In my garden, flowers and vegetables are planted closely together and the distinction between the two is often blurred, making the garden unpretentious and at times even untidy. The flowers and vegetables enjoy each other's shade and support, and since they completely cover the ground, there is no hoeing—although there is some weeding.

When flowers mingle closely with vegetables, the distinction between the two is often blurred; they enjoy each other's shade and support, and since they completely cover the earth, no hoeing and little weeding is required.

The bones of my cutting/kitchen garden were established two decades ago, and have not changed since. The bulk of the garden is divided into 12 rectangular raised beds, each four feet across, and at the entrance to the garden is a circular bed. The beds are small enough that we can reach all the plants without having to step inside and risk compacting the soil. The only straight lines in my garden are the fence and the railroad ties enclosing the raised beds, and sometimes the flowers edging a bed.

The flowers

Vines draw your eyes up, adding a vertical dimension, and giving the garden a finishing touch that other, low-lying plants simply can't provide.

I have planted most of the flowers in clusters as they would be in a border, and placed them where they make the biggest impact; consequently, the front beds are thick with them. As you glance down the main path, you see the ribbons of blooms that dress up the ends of most of the beds. I've placed cascading plants such as nasturtiums and sweet alyssum at the perimeter of the beds to hide the rough edges of the railroad ties. Both can be planted in early April and are undeterred by cold snaps or late frosts. Often they're blooming before I remove the cold frames protecting the tender vegetables and flowers.

The first full bed I plant each April is a mix of salad greens edged with variegated 'Alaska' nasturtiums. The bright flowers spill over the railroad ties and connect the garden to the path. The peppery, speckled leaves of 'Alaska' have become a staple in our salads (they're more flavorful than lettuce). The flowers, too, are edible and can be used as garnishes or in bouquets. Nasturtiums quickly germinate and bloom when direct-seeded in cool weather.

Sweet alyssum is a garden angel. When I need something to edge a bed or fill a gap, I sprinkle alyssum seed in early spring, and it sprouts and blooms as quickly as if it were dropped from heaven. The tiny white flowers seem to froth and foam, sweetly scenting the air.

Shirley poppies, too, are early bloomers that come and go without crowding out others, taking their leave in early summer. They are the most impractical flower for cutting, lasting hardly a weekend in water, but I grow them because their beautiful gossamer petals are heart-stoppers. One seeding of Shirley poppies assures non-stop flowers for at least a month.

The vegetables

Some vegetables need room without competition—tomatoes, zucchini, eggplants, and pumpkins. I leave space between them and cover it with black plastic hidden by salt hay. These plants, too, have flowers around their beds. Signet French marigolds go naturally with tomatoes, since they allegedly frighten the nasty nematodes away. But I like change, so last year brazen purple basil escorted the meek *Laurentia* 'Sophia', with her violet stars, around the tomato cages. Sometimes I surround the zucchini with red gomphrena or 'Red Velvet' celosia, because both flowers are great for drying.

Conversely, a vegetable plant can add a structural element to the flowers. A bed of dahlias is edged with red cabbages, which look like solid wooden beads carved into rosettes and strung into a necklace. Ruffles of green-leaf lettuce boldly planted in clusters alternate with red 'Royal Oak Leaf' lettuce, giving a decorative flounce to a bed.

The herbs

I started by planting the circular bed at the entrance to the garden with only the basic culinary herbs. Over the years, I've added ornamental herbs, scented geraniums, roses, and salvias. Looking for more color among the greens of the herbs, I dressed the center of the herb garden with four 'Simplicity' rose bushes, massing ruffles of sweet alyssum and lavender at their feet. I chose the roses for their strong constitutions, as no chemical sprays are allowed in any of our gardens. Pineapple sage (*Salvia elegans*), another denizen of the circular bed, has pineapple-scented foliage that is flavorful in iced tea and other summer drinks, but I really grow it for its scarlet flowers that bloom in October and November when the rest of the garden is shutting down for the winter.

Many herbs are beautiful enough to jump the fence from the herb garden into the flower border. Lavender and catmint are welcomed everywhere. The flowers of chives I also find beautiful, but because of their onion breath, I leave them behind with the culinary herbs. I planted *Allium aflatunense* 'Purple Sensation' among the chives: the fluffy, light purple balls of chives make the darker purple balls of 'Purple Sensation' jump out and appear taller than their three-foot stems.

The vines

Flowering vines have crept into my garden over the last few years. Vining vegetables and flowering vines twine up and over the fence and up the trellises together. Vines draw your eyes up, adding a vertical dimension to the garden. They do more to give the garden a finishing touch than almost anything else.

It all started with scarlet runner bean, an edible bean with beautiful long-blooming red flowers. The flowers look much like those of sweet peas but without their marvelous scent, and the bloom times of the two plants rarely overlap. Sweet peas should be started indoors under lights in February and planted out in April to bloom in June and July, after which they usually expire from the heat. Scarlet runner beans are direct-seeded in May between the sweet peas, to be harvested later in the summer.

Once I planted one ornamental vine, there was no stopping. What started as a temporary experiment has become permanent. Wooden pyramids, tall ornamental metal columns, and a decorative wooden birdhouse have replaced my original flimsy metal trellises and tepees; these new structures look good even before the vines cover them. The last few years, I've clothed them all with annual flowering vines: morning glories (*Ipomoea purpurea* or *I. tricolor*), climbing snapdragon (*Asarina procumbens*), love-in-a-puff (*Cardiospermum halicacabum*), and Chilean glory vine (*Eccremocarpus scaber*). Cup-and-saucer vine (*Cobaea scandens*), hyacinth bean (*Dolichos lablab* or *Lablab purpureus*), and crimson starglory (*Mina lobata*) are three others that bloom late, at summer's end and after early frost, and make long-lasting cut flowers.

The whole garden is enclosed with a white picket fence and two arbors, one over the entrance gate and the other directly across from it over a garden seat, so I have plenty of places to grow vines. I planted each arbor with climbing roses. In a hurry, we selected our favorites without regard for color: pink 'Aloha', yellow 'Golden Showers', red 'Don Juan' (my favorite for producing edible petals), and multicolored 'Joseph's Coat'. They clash as they climb the arbor, but rather than change them, we named the garden seat the "electric chair" for the jolt of color it delivers.

Before you pull your boots on in the spring to wade through the mud in your kitchen garden, you might want to give the following chapters a read. You'll learn where best to site the garden, how to prepare your soil for planting, and the benefits to both soil and plants of compost and mulches. You'll find a plan for raised beds and a thorough discussion of possible materials for the frame. Succession planting and double cropping will ensure that you have enough of the vegetables, fruits, and herbs that you love, and you'll learn how in "Shortage and Surplus." When your garden closes down again in the late fall, fresh salad greens can be as close as your windowsill, as you'll find in this section, too.

Preparing the Soil for a Kitchen Garden

BY DAYNA S. LANE

A THRIVING, PRODUC-TIVE kitchen garden begins with a healthy, fertile soil. Of course, few of us are blessed with the ideal garden soil. I sure haven't been, even though I have gardened in lots of different places over the years. But soil can be improved. The soil I aim for has an adequate supply of the nutrients plants need, good water-holding capacity and good drainage, and a nice, crumbly structure. Most important, it is a soil that is alive.

A healthy soil teems with life. Soil organisms not only give dirt its rich, earthy aroma, but also drive the dynamics of the soil. Some, such as earthworms, we can see. But it is those we can't see—the microorganisms—that are the most crucial. These organisms perform a myriad of functions, including making nutrients available to plants, and secreting substances that bind soil particles together and create that ideal crumbly structure. One of the most important things a gardener can do to encourage this process is to give the soil regular additions of organic matter.

One of the most important things a gardener can do for the health of his or her kitchen garden is to give the soil regular additions of organic matter.

Texture, structure, and pH

Soil can vary drastically from garden to garden. In one garden I had soil that was so sticky and clayey that after walking around in it I would emerge inches taller. Another was nearly pure beach sand—I almost felt compelled to set up a beach umbrella. The soil in a third garden was a dreadfully compacted alkaline clay with a pH of over 8. (Clay and sand are elements of the texture of the soil, compaction has to do with its structure, and pH is a measurement of its acidity or alkalinity.)

Soil texture is determined by the percentages of the sand, silt, or clay it contains. And the size of these mineral particles directly affects the soil's capacity for holding air, water, and nutrients. Sand, the largest particle, creates good aeration and improves the ability of water to infiltrate the soil. Silt, a smaller particle, has the capacity to hold water so that it's readily available to plants. Clay, by far the smallest particle, holds both nutrients and water well. Fortunately, all three particles are found in most soils. For gardening, a loam soil is considered to have the best proportion of the three, as well as about 5 percent organic matter. Many of us, however, tend to have soils with either a sandy (coarse) texture or, the other extreme, a clayey (fine) texture. Unfortunately, texture is one aspect of soil that is very difficult to change. The amount of sand or clay that most gardeners would have to add to their soils to make a difference would be entirely too large. But adding organic matter can help alleviate the problems of texture extremes, without really changing the texture. By knowing the texture of your soil, you will be better equipped to manage it properly. For instance, sandy soils usually need more water and fertilizer; clay soils are more easily compacted and need more time in the spring to dry out before being worked.

Structure refers to the way soil particles are held together. A soil with good, crumbly structure has adequate pore space for air and water, and for the development of efficient root systems. Good structure can be ruined, though. Frequent foot traffic or heavy equipment can compact soil, for instance. Fortunately, soil structure can be improved with frequent additions of organic matter.

A pH reading tells you how acidic or alkaline your soil is. A reading of 7 is neutral; below 7 is considered acidic, and above 7 is alkaline. The pH of your soil directly affects the availability of nutrients to plants. Most edibles do well within a pH range of 5.5 to 7.5.

It is a good idea to have your soil tested when you begin gardening a new plot and every three to four years after that. A basic soil test kit (available at most garden centers) will test the soil pH and the presence of the major nutrients (nitrogen, phosphorus, and potassium). Many university extension services will test your soil more extensively (including for soil texture, pH, and major and minor nutrients) for a minimal charge.

Preparing the soil

Spring is when most of us get the gardening urge. But before we grab our little red wagons and run around the local nursery picking up lettuce seedlings and pack-

MAKING COMPOST

Compost has so many benefits in the garden that it is sometimes called "black gold." Dark, humus-rich, finished compost can be used as a soil additive or a mulch. Compost's benefits include providing nutrients to plants in a slow-release, balanced fashion; helping break up clay soils; aiding sandy soils in retaining moisture; and correcting pH problems. Other pluses of compost are that it can be made at home and is therefore free, and gives us an excellent way to recycle our yard and kitchen "wastes."

Making compost is simple. You need four major ingredients, well mixed:

1. "Brown" material high in carbon, such as dry leaves, dry grass, other dry garden trimmings, straw, or even shredded black and white newspaper.

2. "Green" material high in nitrogen, such as fresh grass clippings, fresh garden trimmings, kitchen trimmings, or barnyard manures.

3. Water in moderate amounts, so that the mixture is moist but not soggy.

4. Air to supply oxygen to the microorganisms that are doing the decomposition.

Do not add meat, fat, diseased plants, invasive weeds, grasses that reproduce from rhizomes (such as Bermuda grass), or cat or dog manure.

Usually, I don't worry much about the proper proportions, as long as I have a good mix of materials from the garden. However, if the decomposition doesn't seem to be progressing, it is usually because the pile has too much brown (carbon) material, is too dry, or needs air. If the pile smells, it is because it either has too much green (nitrogen) material or is too wet. I bury kitchen trimmings in the pile, so as not to attract flies. The smaller the particles of material and the more often it is turned, the faster it will decompose, sometimes becoming quite hot and steamy. However, it is not mandatory that the compost become hot.

The compost can be in a simple pile or bin or a series of them, on up to rather expensive and elaborate containers. The compost pile or bin should be about 3 feet high and wide and at least 3 feet long (or longer) for the most efficient decomposition and easy workability. In a rainy climate, it's a good idea to have a cover for the compost. My preference is to have two bins. I collect the compost materials in one bin, occasionally sprinkling them with the garden hose and turning to add air. When that bin is full, I turn the contents into the second bin, where it will finish its decomposition. The empty bin is now ready to fill up again with new compostable material.

MULCHING THE KITCHEN GARDEN

An organic mulch benefits a garden in many ways and can save you quite a bit of time, effort, and water. By mulching your kitchen garden, you will conserve moisture, control weeds and soil erosion, moderate soil temperature, and add nutrients and organic matter to the soil. You can use various materials, but homemade compost is usually my first choice. If compost is in short supply, give priority to heavy feeders, like garden peas, that will benefit most from the additional nutrition. Other possible materials include shredded leaves, dried grass clippings, straw, or alfalfa hay. Avoid oat straw, as it may contain oat seeds. If you use straw, you may need to add a nitrogen fertilizer, such as fish meal, as straw will draw nitrogen from the soil. Avoid coarse mulches in moist, shady areas of a garden if slugs are a problem. Keep all mulch 6 to 12 inches away from tree and shrub trunks and about an inch away from the stems of flowers and vegetables.

Some mulches work best in particular situations. For perennial herb beds, use a more permanent mulch such as bark chips or stones. In cold climates, black plastic is useful for warming a seed bed (don't use it around shrubs or trees). Acid-loving plants, like blueberries, benefit from a mulch of pine needles. For paths, woody materials such as sawdust, wood chips, or shredded bark are ideal, as they tie up available nitrogen, therefore suppressing weeds. As a rule, woody materials do not work well as a mulch around vegetables.

ets of carrot seeds, we need to attend to soil preparation. As a rule, soil preparation should start a few days before planting so that there is enough time to do a thorough job. However, you may need to incorporate manure and lime the previous fall.

Gardeners are quite inventive, and there are actually a variety of methods for preparing the soil—everything from the classic "no dig" method, which relies on thick mulches to renew the soil, to the intensive "double-dig" technique. All have their merits, and you should experiment until you find the one that works best for you. The following basic guidelines can help you get started:

Pick an area for your garden that gets at least six hours of sunlight a day (the minimum requirement for most vegetables and herbs). If the lawn needs to be removed, skim off the top layer of sod with a sharp, flat-edged shovel. Some kinds of turf—but definitely not all—can be incorporated back into the soil by chopping it into small pieces (it will need time to decompose), or it can go onto the compost pile for later use. *Do not* incorporate or compost lawn grasses that spread by rhizomes, such as Bermuda grass; remove the sod and as many of the bits and pieces of roots and rhizomes as you can find, and dispose of it all.

Next, turn the soil to remove weeds, rocks, sticks, insect grubs, and other debris. The best tools to use for this task are a garden fork or spade. Do not dig the soil if it is very wet; digging wet soil destroys its structure. On the other hand, if the soil is very hard and dry, moisten it first and then let it drain for a day or more before digging, so that the soil is moist but not soggy.

Unless you are preparing a very large garden or dealing with extremely difficult soil, avoid using a rototiller, as tilling is very hard on soil. Excessive use ruins soil structure, can compact subsoil, and adds too much oxygen to sandy soil, causing organic matter to decompose much too rapidly. If you do use one, be careful not to overuse it, and as time goes by, strive to disturb the soil as little as possible.

Amending the soil

Next, incorporate soil amendments (such as compost, manure, organic fertilizers, or lime) lightly into the top few inches of soil with a garden fork. Add organic matter to the garden on a regular basis. Organic matter is plant or animal material that, when used as a mulch or incorporated into the soil, supplies soil organisms with habitat and food. Beneficial results for the garden are many, including supplying nutrients to plants and improving soil structure. The addition of organic matter will help a sandy soil retain moisture; it will also improve a clay soil's drainage, alleviate compaction, and eventually make it easier to work.

Finished, homemade compost is one of the best organic materials to use (see "Making Compost," page 33). Others include purchased compost, shredded leaves, grass clippings, and green manures. A green manure is a crop grown to be incorporated into the soil; it can be dug directly into the soil (it will need time to decompose) or harvested and composted for later use.

Work the organic matter into the top few inches of soil. How much organic matter you add depends on what type you are using and your soil type. A general rule of thumb is 3 to 6 inches when first beginning a garden and then 1 to 2 inches thereafter per season. Usually, sandy soils need copious amounts, clay soils a more moderate dose, and less for loam. Even with a loam soil, though, and especially when growing vegetables, organic matter and organic fertilizer will need to be added periodically to replenish the soil's vitality.

At the beginning of each season, gently incorporate dry (granular) organic fertilizer into the top 4 to 6 inches of soil. Choose among the very good, all-purpose organic fertilizers on the market today—those having a balanced ratio of the three numbers on every fertilizer package (which stand for nitrogen, phosphorus, and potassium, respectively). Or use an organic fertilizer formulated for the crop you are growing, such as tomato food for tomatoes. Alternatively, you can use individual organic fertilizers, such as blood meal or fish meal for nitrogen, bone meal for phosphorus, and kelp meal for potassium and trace minerals. Follow the fertilizer package directions for recommended amounts to use. Be sure to incorporate phosphorus into the soil where the plant's roots can find it, as phosphorus does not travel through the soil.

Many animal manures are good fertilizers, too—well-aged horse, chicken, rabbit, and steer manure, for example. You can get aged or composted manure by the bag or sometimes by the truckload. If manure is fresh it will need time to decompose before you plant—how long depends on the weather (the warmer the weather, the faster things break down) and the type of manure; allow anywhere from two weeks to three or four months. It is a good idea to compost fresh manure first, before adding it to your garden, or spread it in the fall to be incorporated in the spring. Make sure the manures you use are weed-free, and never use cat or dog manure.

The addition of organic matter on a regular basis will help neutralize an acidic or alkaline soil. If needed, apply lime to raise the pH of acidic soil. It takes time for lime to work, so it is best applied the previous fall. Elemental sulfur lowers the pH of alkaline soil; however, regular addition of organic matter is usually sufficient.

Creating beds

Now you are ready to establish your planting beds. Beds do not have to be in traditional rows. If your garden is on a slope, form the beds perpendicular to the slope. Beds should be no more than 3 to 4 feet wide, so that you can reach the center without walking on them. In areas of high rainfall, a slightly raised bed is sometimes preferable as it drains faster; build up the soil about 4 to 6 inches.

In very arid areas, an ancient technique is to plant in small, rectangular, sunken beds about 6 inches deep, which will not dry out as fast. Whatever your bed type, once the little seedlings get going, mulch the bed to conserve moisture and help control weeds (see "Mulching the Kitchen Garden," p. 34).

Be assured, we gardeners are rewarded for all this attention to the soil. Healthy plants have fewer problems. In the long run, we save time and effort and our kitchen gardens thrive.

Building Raised Beds

BY ROBERT KOURIK

I N MOST KITCHEN GARDENS, planting in raised beds is the best way to ensure healthy plants and an early crop. Raised beds can be simple, double-dug mounds of soil or more formal structures with garden soil enclosed within a framework of wood, masonry, or plastic. The enclosures keep the soil from washing away and help to define the shape of the bed, thus imparting order and efficiency to the garden. There are several other advantages to raised beds: The soil drains better, so plants grow better; in the spring, the soil in raised beds warms slightly earlier; the beds' walls help keep soil or mulch from spilling onto paths; wire mesh can be added to the bottom of a bed to exclude tunneling pests such as moles and gophers; and pathways between beds can be easily cleaned and tended without disturbing plantings.

Raised beds also have some disadvantages. A formal raised bed with solid sides will cost more and require more time and effort to construct than a simple mounded bed. Some gardeners find the angular geometry of raised-bed structures unattractive (though this angularity can be masked with perennial plantings or low evergreens). What's more, if you plan to water your raised bed with drip irrigation, you may want to make an extra effort to bring in the water supply unobtrusively.

Materials

Many types of materials, some recycled, can be used to construct a raised bed. Each has its own benefits and drawbacks, which are outlined below:

Used bricks Old bricks are a good material for raised beds because they are very good-looking and add character to a garden, even when newly built. And since bricks are fairly narrow, the finished wall doesn't take up excess garden space. Wire mesh is also easily added to the bottom. On the other hand, used bricks are expensive, and require some masonry skill or practice to put together. In addition, in areas where the ground freezes, a brick bed will need a concrete base.

Cinder blocks In some cases, cinder blocks can be a good material for raised beds. They are wide enough to sit on while gardening. If unmortared, they are easier to work with than brick; they can be built on a base of packed gravel, and it's easy to add a wire-mesh bottom. They're best used only for square and rectangular beds. The thick blocks take up garden space and look gray and "industrial," like concrete. The large holes in the blocks, usually placed facing up, tend to fill with mulch and soil from the bed. Finally, unless you use mortar and a concrete base, the blocks will often settle in a slightly skewed position.

Plastic "wood" Like lumber, plastic wood is easy to work with—and won't give you splinters. It's made from recycled consumer plastic waste, has a long life, and won't rot. Building oddly angled shapes such as octagons or pentagons is easy with plastic wood, and as with the materials above, it's easy to add a wire-mesh bottom. Up close, though, plastic wood looks very fake. It's also expensive compared to lumber, and requires screws instead of nails for sturdy attachment—a slow and tedious process.

Untreated, rot-resistant lumber The use of the two main rot-resistant lumbers available, redwood and cedar, is controversial. In the West, logging has reduced groves of old-growth, virgin redwood dramatically, and the more

PRESSURE-TREATED WOOD

While tests show that lumber pressure-treated with a solution of chromium, copper, and arsenic (CCA) does not significantly leach these metals into the soil, many food gardeners choose to be cautious and avoid this material for raised beds. If you want to use CCA-treated lumber, the real danger is from direct inhalation and ingestion of the poisonous compounds when sawing the treated wood. Always wear a dust mask and goggles and wash thoroughly immediately after finishing your project.

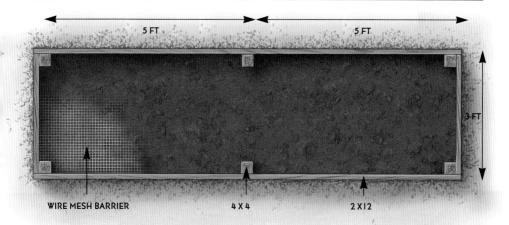

WIRE MESH BARRIER   4 X 4   2 X12

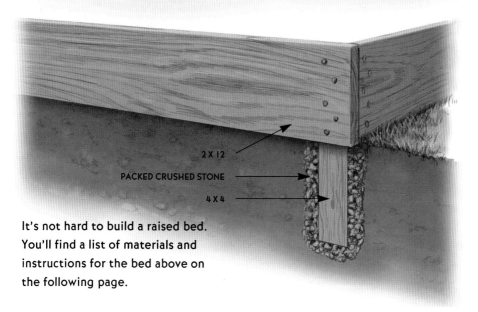

2 X 12

PACKED CRUSHED STONE

4 X 4

It's not hard to build a raised bed. You'll find a list of materials and instructions for the bed above on the following page.

pervasive harvesting of second-growth redwood—as well as virgin and replanted cedar—raises concerns about renewable forestry. Using recycled wood lessens the environmental impact. The major drawback of using wood is its propensity to rot over time. Redwood heartwood can last up to two decades, but white redwood sapwood usually rots within four years and should be avoided. Untreated pine or Douglas fir lumber may last only two to five years, depending on whether your climate is wet and humid or arid. Wood, however, is still the easiest material for building raised beds. It is a good-looking natural surface. It's easy to work with; no mask, gloves, or goggles are required when using hand tools. Beds with odd-angled

Planting in enclosed raised beds is the best way to ensure healthy plants and an early crop, to keep the soil from washing away, and to define the shape of the beds.

shapes can be constructed from wood. It is also easy to add a wire-mesh bottom to wooden beds.

Construction Of all the materials available, wood is still the first choice for many gardeners. Here's how to install a 3-foot-wide by 10-foot-long by 12-inch-high wooden (or plastic "wood") raised bed on level ground:

Materials:

• Six 4" x 4" posts (4" x 4"s as sold in lumberyards are actually 3½" x 3½"), each cut to 24" long.

• Two 2" x 12" boards (actually 1½" x 11¼" wide), cut to 10' long.

• Two 2" x 12" boards (actually 1½" x 11¼" wide), cut to 33" long.

• (Optional) a 4' x 11' piece of ½" wire mesh (aviary wire).

• Several dozen 10 d or 12 d (d stands for "penny") hot-dipped galvanized box nails; these textured nails will help hold the wood together and the texture helps keep board-ends from splitting.

Level the entire 3-foot by 10-foot bed area, plus a bit into the pathways. Check that all is flat by setting a carpenter's level on a long 2" x 4" and taking readings at various points across and along the area. Measure and make marks in the soil where the four corner posts and the two midpoint posts (see diagram) will be. The marks at the ends of the beds should be 29½ inches apart (the 3-foot width minus the width of two 1½-inch thick side boards, and half the thickness of the corner posts). Along the length, make the marks for the end posts 113½ inches apart (to accommodate the overlap of the 33-inch ends and half of the thickness of the posts).

Excavate a 12-inch-deep or deeper hole for each of the six supporting posts. (Some gardeners don't put the posts in the ground, but use the 4 x 4s as blocking for constructing a box that rests on the surface. With this method, however, the weight of soil in the bed may buckle the sides outward.) Put the posts into the holes and add just enough ½-inch crushed rock mixed with dust and soil to hold them upright.

Double-check all measurements between the posts by checking to make sure the bed is square: (a) add string along all sides of the posts and use the three-foot end as one side of a 3' x 4' x 5' triangle; (b) measure from the corner along one of the ten-foot sides to a point on the string four feet from the corner; (c) measure diagonally from this point to the other end of the three-foot side. If the sides are square, the length of the diagonal measurement will be five feet.

Add more crushed rock to the top of each hole, using the level to make sure each post is vertical. Tamp around each post with an iron bar to compact the gravel. (Cement may be used instead of gravel with plastic "wood," but solid wooden posts set in cement will rot much more quickly than in well-tamped gravel.) If you have burrowing pests, lay the ½-inch wire mesh over the entire bed area. Cut the wire mesh to fit tightly around the base of each post.

Attach the boards as shown in the diagram; begin by hammering the first nail into each board near the bottom. Check the level of the board at the opposite end, and nail that end in place. Hammer a nail into the board every 3 inches up the post. (Only screws will secure plastic wood to the posts. Because plastic wood doesn't give way to a screw as easily as wood grain, all holes must be pre-drilled with an electric drill. Drill one hole so the shank of the screw can pass cleanly through the 2-inch thick board. Then pre-drill another hole in the post small enough in diameter to hold onto the screws' threads.)

Cut the tops of all posts off at a 45-degree angle down toward the interior of the box so they won't show when the bed is filled with soil. Use staples to attach the bottom wire flush every 2 inches.

Add your favorite blend of garden soil, topsoil, and compost. You're ready to plant!

Shortage and Surplus in the Kitchen Garden

BY DOC AND KATY ABRAHAM

OST PEOPLE WHO PUT IN a kitchen garden are benign "gamblers." They either produce a surplus or a shortage of food. Of course, the stakes aren't earth-shattering, but it can be frustrating. With a little planning before you plant, you can come out with an amount fairly close to what you need, barring unforeseen circumstances.

Home gardens today are not as large as they used to be. Years ago, it was estimated that to produce enough vegetables for a family of four you would need a garden plot 150 feet wide by 50 feet long. But this isn't a fair estimate for today's gardens, which are often much smaller, grown "vertically" on stakes, trellises, or fences, or in containers. Fortunately, new space-saving vegetable varieties have been developed, so we can now have more plants in less space. But planning is still important; you'll be disappointed if you go through a lot of work and effort and end up raising only enough lettuce for one salad, or enough pea pods for one stir-fry.

Grow popular vegetables

The first step in avoiding surplus or shortage is to get the family in on deciding what to grow. What does everyone like the most (or the least)? Few kids would vote for okra, salsify (vegetable oyster), or turnips, but they may love cherry tomatoes, strawberries, and fresh peas. Or maybe there's something you all like but don't eat very often. If you seldom use acorn squash in cooking, why grow it? Do you eat Mexican food frequently? Then be sure to put in plenty of

Make your kitchen garden beautiful as well as bountiful by planting a few decorative varieties. You may not want to devote a lot of space to spinach, for example, when you can grow rainbow-hued Swiss chard and use it in more dishes. And always go heavy on the standards—tomatoes, lettuce, beans, peas, carrots—and other family favorites.

tomatoes, hot peppers, onions, and cilantro. Always go heavy on the standards—tomatoes, lettuce, beans, peas, carrots—and other family favorites. And since a kitchen garden should be beautiful as well as bountiful, why not choose a few decorative varieties? For instance, you may not want to devote a lot of space to spinach when you can grow colorful Swiss chard and use it in more dishes.

One of the primary benefits of growing your own food is getting that delectable, fresh-off-the-vine flavor that you rarely get with supermarket produce—and getting it more cheaply, too. But if it's just as easy to buy fresh, locally grown sweet corn or strawberries at a nearby farmer's market, then perhaps you don't need to grow your own.

Try to fill your kitchen garden with varieties that are not easy to buy locally, that everyone in your family will want to eat, that you can use in a variety of recipes, and that will be attractive additions to the garden. All these things will save labor and space, and prevent waste.

Optimize your space

Succession planting and double cropping can help you grow enough of whatever you need in your kitchen garden. Some vegetables mature fast enough to be removed early in the season. These can be followed by another sowing of the same vegetable, or of any other vegetable that will have time to mature. Our family has always been fond of green beans. After the first crop of beans is through producing, we sow them again to stretch the season. This is called "succession planting." When the second crop has been harvested, we pull up the plants and sow two cool-weather crops, turnips and Swiss chard. This is called "double cropping."

Other crops that are out of the way in time to be followed by another crop include early cabbage, lettuce, peas, beets, radishes, carrots, turnips, spinach, and scallions. Lettuce and radishes are especially short-lived in the garden. You get more mileage from these by pulling up the mature plants after harvesting and planting a fresh crop. You can even do this with early corn if Jack Frost doesn't interfere in early fall.

How much to plant?

Ordering seeds to plant a kitchen garden for a family of four is difficult because seed companies do not package their seeds that way. The chart on page 45 gives rough estimates for how far a certain amount of seed will go. From there, you'll have to do a little math to determine what you need to plant for your size garden. For example, if a half pound of corn seed will plant a 500-foot row, a quarter pound will plant a 250-foot row, and so on. If you have a 50-foot row, you'll need close to 2 ounces of seed.

HOW MUCH SEED?		
	AMT.	YIELD
Asparagus	1 pkt.	50 ft. row
Beans, bush	½ lb.	50 ft. row
Beans, pole	½ lb.	50 "hills"
Beets	1 oz.	20 ft. row
Broccoli	1 pkt.	12 plants
Brussels sprouts	1 pkt.	12 plants
Cabbage, early	1 pkt.	8 plants
Cabbage, late	1 pkt.	8 plants
Carrots	½ lb.	15 ft. row
Cauliflower	1 pkt.	10 ft. row
Corn, early	½ lb.	60 ft. row
Corn, late	½ lb.	60 ft. row
Cucumbers	1 pkt.	20 "hills"
Eggplant	1 pkt.	10 plants
Endive	1 pkt.	20 ft. row
Lettuce, head	1 pkt.	20 ft. row
Lettuce, leaf	1 pkt.	10 ft. row
Muskmelon	1 pkt.	10 "hills"
Watermelon	1 pkt.	8 "hills"
Onion seed	½ oz.	25 ft. row
Onion sets	1 lb.	25 ft. row
Onion plants	100	35 ft. row
Parsley	1 pkt.	15 ft. row
Parsnips	1 pkt.	20 ft. row
Peas	½ lb.	40 ft. row
Peppers	1 pkt.	36 plants
Radishes	1 pkt.	10 ft. row
Spinach	1 oz.	20 ft. row
Squash, summer	1 pkt.	15 ft. row
Squash, winter	1 pkt.	15 ft. row
Swiss chard	1 pkt.	15 ft. row
Tomatoes	1 pkt.	36 plants

Surplus is better than shortage

If you must err, do so on the side of surplus rather than shortage. Problems with weather, insects, nibbling rabbits, and gardener error will always conspire to do away with all or part of your crop, so it's better to plant more than you think you'll need than to plant too little. The old rule of thumb is "plant one for the bugs, one for the deer, and one for yourself." But don't forget that other old rule of thumb: "Don't bite off more than you can chew."

Having a surplus is one thing; letting things go to waste is quite another. Today's busy families may have a hard time keeping up with the harvesting, and may find much of their garden produce being wasted. Radishes get hard and pithy if they overripen. Lettuce bolts, or goes to seed, if not picked daily. Cucumbers turn yellow, and the vines dry up. Corn, peas, and beans get hard if not picked when tender. Scallions turn yellow and form bulbs unless they are harvested regularly. Even tomatoes should be watched on the vine and picked when the fruit starts to turn red all over (but not bloody red). Most vegetables should be collected at the peak of ripeness and not left to overripen on the plant. If you're not ready to use them at that time, many can be stored for future

One of the main benefits of growing your own food is that fresh-off-the-vine flavor you rarely get with supermarket produce.

Few kids would vote to include okra, salsify, or turnips in the garden, but they may love cherry tomatoes, strawberries—and fresh peas.

use, and others can be preserved or frozen in some way.

Regardless of how well you plan it, you're bound to have a bumper crop in some years. Even if you can't use it all or preserve it all, you can make an effort to give it away to those who need it. The Garden Writers Association of America (GWAA) has a program called "Plant a Row for the Hungry," which provides a way to distribute excess garden produce to people in need. (To find out more, contact the GWAA at 703-257-1032). There are also people in just about every neighborhood who used to be gardeners but, due to age or infirmity, are no longer able to keep it up. Those of us who are able can bring a lot of joy to these people by giving them our extra plants or vegetables. And don't forget to give surplus seeds and plants to school kids, church groups, Boy Scouts, and correctional facilities. A surplus is always better than a shortage.

An Indoor Salad Garden

BY LUCY APTHORP LESKE

 INTER SALADS ALWAYS SEEM blander than summer salads, at least here in the Northeast where I live—despite advances in commercial growing techniques and the increased availability of fresh produce at the market year-round. However, with ingenuity and planning, it is possible to grow a few things indoors in cold regions of the country to add zing to winter salads.

Choice plants for indoors

Many greens take to indoor winter culture, including lettuce, mesclun, beets, chard, and mustard. These plants are easily adaptable to containers and they grow quickly. They tolerate the low light levels and cold temperatures of winter windowsills, and they will even forgive you if you neglect them a bit. The trick is

47

Choose salad varieties for your windowsill garden that mature in 30 to 60 days, because, if planted in late December through March, they'll be ready to harvest between late January and April.

to grow plants from seed to a size big enough to make a difference in a salad; in other words, halfway between sprouts and the real thing.

Which vegetables grow best depends to some degree on daylength. Plants that prefer the short days and cool nights of spring and fall are the ones most likely to thrive indoors in winter—plants like beets, spinach, spring and fall lettuce, and other related greens. Plants that prefer long days either will be stimulated to flower and bolt, thus producing tough, bitter leaves, or will grow too slowly. Also, varieties that are suitable for cut-and-come-again culture are preferable to those that produce tight or compact heads that can only be harvested once.

Varieties that require 30 to 60 days to maturity are best suited for indoor culture because, if planted in late December through March, they are ready to harvest between late January and April. It would be a waste of space and time to sow crops that need more than 60 days to mature; by the time they are ready to harvest, the outdoor garden can be producing. More important, low light levels and indoor conditions cause plants to grow more slowly than they would outdoors. Days to maturity—the average length of time for a plant to reach mature size—signifies whether or not a variety is a fast grower. This is usually indicated on the seed packet.

Spring and fall leaf lettuces, like oakleaf, buttercrunch, and looseleaf, are ideal indoor crops because they meet all of the above requirements. Days to maturity range from 45 to 60, and the plants resprout vigorously from cut stems. Any variety will do, including the various spring and fall leaf-lettuce mixes available from seed catalogs.

Mesclun is also suitable for indoor culture because it grows well in containers and in small quantities adds concentrated bursts of flavor and nutrition to salads. Mesclun greens include wild and cultivated plants like chicory, cress, chervil, lettuce, dandelion, arugula, endive, purslane, orach, fennel, and others.

In addition, beet and chard greens, mustard, and cress produce leaves large enough for a salad four to six weeks after sowing. All are suitable for cut-and-come-again culture and will continue to produce leaves after the initial cutting for several more weeks. After leaves have been harvested two or three times, cut the plants off at the surface, and sow a new crop.

Light and temperature requirements

What plants to grow and how many depends on how much space you have. Obviously, the more light plants get, the faster they grow. Fluorescent grow lights are best, but if that's not practical or possible, windowsills work, too—if they provide the minimum four hours of sunlight per day that indoor salad plants require to thrive. Here in the Northeast, the strongest winter light comes from eastern and southern exposures; north of New Jersey, western exposures tend to provide fairly weak light levels in the afternoons.

There must be enough light to prevent unhealthy nitrogen buildup in the leaves. Research has shown that salad greens grown under low light conditions can develop high nitrate levels, and this can have deleterious health effects if the greens are eaten in sufficient quantity. The four hours of daily sunlight that plants need is also enough to prevent nitrogen from accumulating in the foliage.

Temperature also affects how well the plants grow. Most of the plants recommended above can tolerate the cold, drafty conditions of winter windowsills quite well—even as low as 40° F. at night and 60° F. during the day. Beets, chard, mustard, and hardy varieties of mesclun will even tolerate freezing temperatures. What most of these crops can't stand is heat and low humidity, so they should not be grown near a wood stove or on a windowsill over a radiator.

Materials you'll need

Indoor salad gardens do not require fancy equipment to be successful. The basic materials needed are a supply of seeds, clean containers, sterile soilless potting mix, a source of water, and a source of nutrients. Four to six packets of seed are usually enough to supplement salads for a family of four from December through April.

The size and type of container can be as varied as the crops. Cut-and-come-again greens can be sown in windowboxes, while beets and chard, with their long taproots, should be sown in deeper, standard pots. Clay pots are better for cold windowsill environments because clay retains some warmth in the evening and keeps the soil from getting soggy. Plastic is better for warm, dry environments because it helps the potting mix retain more moisture. Whatever shape the container, it should be able to fit on the windowsill with a drip-proof tray secured snugly underneath.

To reduce the possibility of disease, all containers must be cleaned and sterilized—especially if they were used outdoors the previous summer—and filled with sterile soilless potting mix. As the seedlings begin to grow, feed them with a soluble fertilizer such as Squanto's fish fertilizer.

Windowsill harvest time

Depending on the variety, harvest time runs from several weeks to several months. Some plants, like mustard, are best when they are only a few weeks old; the tiny plants are deliciously pungent. Others, like lettuce, are better when they have some size. In general, start harvesting when the leaves are big enough not to slip through the tines of a fork. Stop harvesting when the plants turn yellow, stop growing, or begin to produce flowers, whichever comes first.

Harvest indoor salad plants by cutting the leaves with scissors rather than pulling them. Because indoor salad plants are planted more closely than they are in the garden, pulling upsets the soil, and usually more than one plant comes up at a time. Once a crop has exhausted its potential to produce more leaves, I simply cut it off at the soil surface and sow another crop.

Don't be fooled by appearances. Windowsill greens tend to be floppier and scrawnier than their spring and summer cousins. They still taste great—far better than the grocery-store alternatives.

PLANTING THE GARDEN

One of the greatest pleasures of kitchen gardening is thinking about which vegetables, fruits, herbs, and flowers to nurture and enjoy through the coming seasons. You can choose from among a seemingly infinite variety of plants, each with its own taste, look, and growth habits.

In the following pages, expert kitchen gardeners divulge their favorite plants for the kitchen garden—compact vegetables for the mini-kitchen garden, heirloom plants that taste great and help preserve biodiversity, plants that produce flowers that taste good enough to eat, and fruits that will grace your garden without shading out your other crops.

⚎

Essential Plants for the Gourmet Kitchen Garden

BY RENEE SHEPHERD

ITCHEN GARDENS SHOULD BE planned around the vegetables and herbs you enjoy most at the table. Think about what you love to eat throughout the growing season to find out what you'll want to plant in abundance. Add a few specialties you love that might be difficult to find in the grocery store—for me, that means chili peppers for making delicious Mexican dishes. Also consider which vegetables and herbs you may want to grow in quantity to freeze or dry for the cold winter months. Plan to grow a good selection of your favorite herbs to add savor to everyday meals and preserve for year-round use as well. A few edible flowers are also welcome additions to the kitchen garden. Herb and flower blossoms will help attract pollinators to make all your plants more fruitful, and a good mix of plants will also welcome beneficial insects to the garden; diversity always adds to the garden's overall health.

Here are some of my own choices for kitchen garden "essentials"—plants I wouldn't be without and look forward to growing each and every season. I've included both early, cool-season plants to harvest in late spring and warm-season fruiting plants for summer. In milder climates like mine (I live in Felton, California, just south of San Francisco in Zone 8), you can also plant cool-season crops again in late summer for continuous autumn harvests. These easy-to-grow favorites will produce beautiful big harvests to reward you for your gardening labors of love.

At maturity, peppers ripen to red, orange, gold, or even a rich chocolate, like these 'Chocolate Beauties' (left). Peppers taste sweeter and juicier at this mature stage and are chock-full of sugars and vitamins, especially vitamin C.

Baby pac choi, an early cool-season crop, has meltingly tender flesh that will become a real craving you'll want to satisfy every season.

Heirloom lemon cucumbers are crunchy, sweet, and good fresh or pickled, and they come in just two months after planting.

Early/cool-season plants

Baby mesclun salad mixes Savoring the first succulent leaves of spring salads is a great way to welcome the new season, and the kitchen gardener's spring tonic. "Mesclun" is a French term for early mixed young salad plants of many kinds. In the U.S., mesclun has come to mean a whole range of mixed young greens. It includes lettuces of all the different colors—light and dark green, burgundy, pink, and pale lime—as well as several different leaf shapes and textures. Mesclun may also incorporate other, more piquant greens with frilly notched leaves such as tangy arugula, endive, and kale; bright green sweet mizuna; and leafy mustard. You can buy mesclun seed mixes already made up or mix up your own by combining different lettuces and early greens. I recommend using the premade mixtures seed companies offer because the varieties in them have been selected to grow at a similar rate, and the colors, tastes, and textures of the mix have been balanced.

Mesclun mix makes it easy to grow a gourmet's palette for the salad bowl, and these pretty mixes create a mosaic of color in the spring garden. Plant them

Harvest pepper fruits, like these 'Corno di Toro', when they are fully colored by cutting, not pulling, them at the stem.

by the "cut and come again" method in early spring as soon as the soil can be worked. To do this, simply sow the seed thickly in a wide row or 3' x 3' area of finely worked, well-drained soil. Let the seed fall from your loosely cupped hand by shaking it out the way you would cover a cake with candy sprinkles. Cover lightly, water gently, and keep moist. Let the seedlings grow without thinning. In just 40 to 50 days they will carpet the garden bed and reach 4 to 5 inches tall.

Harvest at this height by cutting the leaves with scissors, leaving the plant crowns about one inch tall to regrow for another harvest. Voila! You've got a pretty baby salad mix as fancy as anything you'd get in an upscale restaurant. Best of all, your mesclun bed will regrow for another harvest or two if you keep the crowns watered and feed them with fish emulsion or manure tea. Plan to sow another bed a few weeks after your first planting for the longest succession of harvest.

These spring greens will be sweet and meltingly tender. Use them promptly, adding a sprinkling of your favorite fresh herbs. Avoid heavy dressings that can overwhelm the baby leaves' delicate taste and texture. A sprinkling of good extra-virgin olive oil and a little balsamic vinegar, along with a few grinds of fresh pepper, sets them off splendidly. I like to toss in some toasted pine nuts and a handful of freshly grated Asiago cheese; the result is a truly sumptuous salad.

Rainbow-hued Swiss chard Chard, with its big leafy stalks, is a terrific spring and early summer vegetable because it is versatile, healthy, and tastes good—and is very ornamental. Very young leaves are good for salads, and as plants grow to maturity they provide months of substantial cooked greens. Chard is delicious steamed, stir-fried, used in casseroles like spinach, or simply braised in broth and served with a bit of fresh lemon juice and olive oil. These

Grow at least three tomato plants, each with different colored fruits so you can enjoy the range of their appeal. These 'Sungold' cherry tomatoes are a sweet treat.

large-framed plants hold up well in the garden, and in mild winter climates, chard will overwinter handily.

There are many varieties of chard with green leaves and stalks and pretty red chard with red stalks and red-veined green leaves. My own favorite is an old heirloom that comes in a true rainbow of colors—the leaves are green, but the stalks and leaf veins are a mixture of crimson, gold, yellow, orange, pink, and pale lime. The effect is show-stopping in the garden. This chard, sold by several varietal names ('Jacobs Coat', 'Bright Lights', 'Rainbow'), is particularly sweet and delicious with no metallic aftertaste.

Plan to direct-sow chard in a sunny spot in well-prepared soil in early spring, or start seedlings indoors in containers to transplant as soon as they have several sets of true leaves. You can begin harvesting when plants have six to eight leaves, letting new ones grow as replacements. Plants will bear for months if not over-harvested. Feed once a month with a well-balanced fertilizer.

Chard is a garden staple that goes well with rice, pasta, and potatoes. Try slowly sautéing some garlic, mashing in a few anchovies, and a pinch or two of dried chile flakes. Then add a big bunch of chopped chard leaves and some chicken broth and a little white wine. Cook until chard is tender, then toss with freshly cooked hot pasta and top with grated hard cheese. Simple preparations like this demonstrate the many ways fresh chard makes a delectable and savory addition to everyday cooking.

Baby pac choi Everyone who loves stir-fry will delight in the sweet, mild flavor of baby pac choi. It is tender and delicious, and so mild that it makes a fine crispy steamed vegetable cooked all by itself. Baby pac choi plants are a very early and quick cool-season crop for early spring (and again for a late summer or early fall crop). In the cool weather of the beginning gardening season, it will be ready to eat and fully harvested in just 45 days, well in time to use the same space for summer fruiting plants like tomatoes or peppers.

My favorite variety is 'Mei Qing Choi', whose pastel, mint-green stalks form graceful little vase-shaped plants topped with broad, oval, rich green leaves. The sturdy 6- to 8-inch-tall plants with their slightly glossy leaves are tolerant of both cold and heat and have a succulent, crispy texture.

You can sow seed directly in the prepared garden bed or transplant seedlings to about 6 inches apart. 'Mei Qing Choi' grows easily in rich soil if kept evenly moist. If you thin young plants, the thinnings make very tender, quick-cooking morsels. When mature, harvest the entire plants, which will look like little green bouquets.

Stir-fry quickly for any Oriental-style dish, or quickly sauté or steam the stalks and serve with ham or sausages. 'Mei Qing Choi' has meltingly tender flesh, never strong or cabbagy tasting. Its fresh flavor will become a real craving you'll want to satisfy every season. A natural for the healthy table, pac choi is a member of the cancer-preventing, heart-healthy *Brassica* genus (along with broccoli, cabbage, cauliflower, and others). After you've enjoyed the harvest, turn the soil, add compost, and plant your heat-loving summer vegetables.

Spinach Freshly grown spinach, picked young and tender, bears little comparison to the strong-flavored, tougher supermarket product. Garden spinach has a buttery, full flavor, never too overwhelming or metallic in taste. Use it fresh-picked in salads, spinach borscht, or gently steamed just until the leaves softly wilt. Old-fashioned creamed spinach made with your own spring or fall crop can't be surpassed. Spinach is a real cool-season, early spring or late fall crop because it doesn't tolerate hot weather well. Look for smooth-leafed varieties as they are easier to clean. My favorites are 'Nordic', 'Wolter', 'Olympia', 'Spice', and 'Tyee', a semi-smooth variety that is slow to bolt.

Sow the big seeds directly into the garden as soon as the soil can be worked, and be sure to firm the soil well over the seeds. Keep the seed bed evenly moist, and expect somewhat uneven germination. It's fine to resow if some of your spinach doesn't come up, as new plants will catch up easily. You can thin plants

Nothing satisfies the gardening cook like the pleasure of harvesting big baskets of richly ripe, juicy tomatoes. 'Green Zebra', (above) is gold and green when ripe.

to 2 to 4 inches apart (thinnings are delicious) and harvest individual leaves as the plants mature. The shiny, dark green leaves are very ornamental in the garden. When the weather begins to get seriously hot and your spinach bed threatens to bolt, shear it all back and enjoy a big fresh salad.

Try fresh spinach with an old-fashioned hot bacon dressing and grated hardboiled eggs, or make a dressing flavored with curry or a spoonful of peanut butter for something a little different. Fresh spinach salad is also delicious with sweet onion and red apple slices. When you have a good crop, make a spinach soufflé for a special occasion or eggs Florentine for a wonderful spring brunch.

Warm-season plants

Tomatoes Nothing satisfies the gardening cook like the pleasure and satisfaction of harvesting big baskets of richly ripe, juicy tomatoes. Plan to grow at least three plants, each with different colored fruits so you can enjoy the full range of their appeal. Many garden centers sell only red-fruited varieties, so you may have to start from seed to get diversity.

To grow from seed, tomatoes need to be started indoors six weeks before night temperatures rise into the 50° F range. They need this head start if they are to grow to maturity and bear good harvests before temperatures begin to cool down and days grow shorter in fall. Seeds need a fine seed-starting mix to grow in and warm, 80° to 85° F. temperatures to germinate promptly. Just as soon as they emerge, seedlings need lots of light. Once seedlings have several sets of true leaves, transplant them to 4-inch containers and feed once every two weeks with a half-strength fertilizer solution. Be sure to give them a very bright windowsill or, better yet, keep them close under fluorescent lights. When the weather outside is warm both day and night, it's time to set the plants into rich, well-amended garden soil in a sunny spot, about 3 feet apart. Provide stakes or trellises, for tomato vines grow into big, heavy plants.

I like indeterminate varieties, which keep growing and producing over a long season. Mulch young plants to help provide the consistent soil moisture plants prefer. Fruits will begin to ripen by midsummer. Don't worry if the first ripe tomatoes are a little bland; full flavor develops after the earliest fruits come on.

For best taste and texture, don't refrigerate your ripe tomatoes. The cold temperatures will mute their sweet, full flavor. If you have a real abundance, freeze them in plastic freezer bags to use later—they'll lose shape and texture, but still taste delicious in cooked dishes or made into sauce next winter. One of my favorite simple ways to enjoy freshly ripe tomatoes is to slice up several of them in different colors and arrange them in overlapping slices on a big platter with some crumbled feta or fresh mozzarella cheese in the center. Then I sprinkle with fruity olive oil and a pinch of coarse salt, and garnish with green and purple basil. For a

---

FAVORITE TOMATO VARIETIES

Classic red tomatoes:
  'Brandywine'
  'Carmello'
  'Celebrity'
  'Dona'
  'Early Girl'
  'Enchantment'
Multicolored tomatoes:
  'Green Zebra' or 'Green Grapes'—golden overlaid with green striping
  'Old Flame' or 'Striped German'—pink-red and gold
  'Black Russian'—red overlaid with purple-black
Gold and orange tomatoes:
  'Lemon Boy'—sunny yellow
  'Persimmon'—rich orange
  'Mandarin Cross'—deep golden orange
  'Sungold'—orange cherry
  'Valencia'—bright orange

Pick squash when very young for best tenderness and taste—about 2 inches across for scallop squash such as these 'Peter Pan Green Scallops'.

symphony of color and flavor, nothing can beat this for a summer lunch with a loaf of crusty French bread!

Sweet bell peppers Most of us grew up eating green peppers, but green is actually their immature stage—all peppers ripen in maturity to red, orange, gold, or even a rich chocolate, depending on the variety. They taste sweeter and juicier at this mature stage and are chock-full of sugars and vitamins, especially vitamin C. Plan to grow several varieties that mature to different hues so you can experience their full range of colors.

Pepper seeds must be started indoors, just like tomatoes, except that they demand consistent warmth—germination is best at 85°-90° F. Be sure to wait until the weather is warm and settled and above 50° F. both day and night before planting seedlings out. Set peppers 1½ to 2 feet apart. Pepper plants are very ornamental with pretty blossoms, so put them in the front of the garden. Many vigorous varieties will need staking since they grow into big-framed plants with heavy fruit sets. Mulch the plants when they are about 6 inches tall, and feed at least once a month with a well-balanced fertilizer for best production. Harvest fruits when they are fully colored (or before the first fall frost, whichever comes first) by cutting them at the stem; pulling them off will tear the plant. Keep ripe fruits picked to encourage production.

Ripe peppers are delicious simply sliced up and slowly sautéed in a bit of olive oil with garlic and garnished with fresh basil. Or sprinkle pepper strips with oil and grill them to develop a delicious sweetness. Make your own fajitas with barbecued beef or chicken strips and peppers folded into flour tortillas with salsa and cilantro, or try a tuna salad with fresh, juicy sweet pepper strips, capers, and olives.

Hot chile peppers Hot peppers or chiles grow just like sweet bell peppers. Plan to grow several plants for making your own fresh salsa; they'll be ripe just when your tomatoes are peaking. Many chiles dry easily, or you can freeze them for year-round use. Grow a mild variety like 'Anaheim' or 'Poblano' for everyday cooking or stuffing; a plant of medium heat for salsa, like 'Jalapeno' or 'Numex'; they'll be ripe just when your tomatoes are peaking. Many chiles dry easily, or you can freeze them for year-round use.

Chile plants are very handsome garden additions. They will produce heavy crops beginning in midsummer, and fruits that hang like ornaments on the plants. They hold well and can be harvested at either the green or mature red stage. Remember to cut, not pull, pods from plants.

To use chiles, first char-roast them over an open flame or broiler, then cool and peel and seed them. (Always wear gloves when handling chiles). Add roasted, peeled chiles to corn, beans, squash, or tomatoes for new flavor combinations. Try your hand at making chile pickles or cheese-stuffed chile "poppers." Use some fresh pods to flavor vinegar and sherry for tasty condiments. With your own abundant crops, you'll be able to experiment in the kitchen and make lots of great spicy dishes from a wide range of Thai, Chinese, Mexican, Caribbean, African, and Indian cuisines.

Summer squash Enjoy the nutty flavor of the best summer squash at the baby stage. Grow several different kinds so you'll have both a green- and a yellow-fruiting plant; zucchini, crookneck, or pattypan types are equally easy to grow.

Seed for all kinds of summer squashes should be sown directly in the garden when temperatures both night and day are evenly in the 50° F. range and weather is warm and sunny. Plant 3 feet apart in hills with lots of added compost or well-rotted manure. Thin seedlings gradually to the one or two best plants. Marauding birds love to destroy squash seedlings, so a good trick is to cover young seedlings with plastic strawberry baskets to foil them. Remove when plants crowd the baskets.

Most newer summer squash varieties start producing in just 6 to 7 weeks. Pick the fruit very young for best tenderness and taste—this means about 2 inches across

---

FAVORITE SQUASH VARIETIES

Scalloped:
  'Sunburst Golden Scallops'
  'Peter Pan Green Scallops'
Crookneck:
  'Supersett'
  'Sundance'
  'Dixie'
Zucchini:
  'Arlesa'
  'Raven'
  'Ambassador'
  'Condor'
  'Clarimore'

Plant purple beans, such as these 'Royal Burgundy', for a joyous display—and you'll easily find the bright-colored pods at harvest-time.

for scallop squash and no more than 4 to 5 inches long for zucchini and crookneck types. Young squash are really succulent and can be quickly steamed (but don't overcook!) and sprinkled with your favorite fresh herbs and a little butter for a scrumptious summer vegetable. I like summer squash tossed with either chopped parsley, dill, garlic chives, or lemon thyme. One of my favorite recipes is baby squash steamed with tiny carrots and pearl onions, topped with chopped fresh dill. Don't forget the squash blossoms, which can be stuffed and baked or sautéed. I like to fill them with a mixture of ricotta cheese, basil, parsley, grated cheese, and toasted almonds; or stir-fry quartered baby squashes with blossoms still attached with snow peas and red pepper strips for a beautiful presentation.

Snap beans Crisp green beans are one of the easiest and most reliable kitchen-garden plants. Freshly grown and harvested, they are juicy with delicate sweet flavor that can't be duplicated. Plan to grow some purple and yellow as well as green-podded varieties for a joyous display and because the bright-colored pods are easy to find on the plants at harvest time. I always sow both bush beans, which come on with their harvest first, and pole beans, which vine up tall stakes and provide full abundance later in summer when the bush beans are finished bearing.

Sow beans 2 to 3 inches apart in wide rows when the weather is warm and summery. Be sure to protect young seedlings from birds, who love to pull them up. If you don't get a strong stand from your first sowing, plant again since young seedlings will catch up quickly. Provide 8- to 10-foot stakes for vining pole varieties at the time of planting. Keep seedlings evenly moist, but to avoid spreading disease, don't work in the bean patch when plants are wet.

Delicate young beans can be quickly cooked to the tender-crisp stage in boiling salted water, cooled in ice water, then reheated with your favorite herbs or served

---

FAVORITE PEPPER VARIETIES

Red when mature:
  'Vidi'
  'Northstar'
  'Lipstick'
  'Cadice'
  'Figaro'—flattened pimento type
Gold or orange when mature:
  'Valencia'—orange
  'Quadrato d'Oro'—golden yellow
  'Orobelle'—golden yellow
  'Queen'—deep orange
  'Corno di Toro'—gold or red when mature, elongated shape
  'Ivory'—creamy pastel yellow
Chocolate-colored when mature:
  'Chocolate Beauty'

FAVORITE CHILE VARIETIES

Mild:
  'Anaheim'
  'Ancho' or 'Poblano'
  'Pasilla'
  'Ortega'
Medium hot:
  'Numex'
  'Early' or 'Tam Jalapes'
  'Mirasol'
Spicy hot:
  'Serrano'
  'Cayenne'
  'Superchili'
  'Bulgarian Carrot'
  'Habaarian'
  'Tabasco'
  'Thai Dragon'

---

at room temperature with vinaigrette. I sauté these blanched beans in a little olive oil with green olives, lemon, garlic, parsley, and toasted pecans or walnuts. It's also easy to blanch and freeze beans for winter use. Or try your hand at making dilly bean pickles! Cooked green beans are also delicious blended into green bean pâté.

Lemon cucumbers These American heirlooms are my favorite cucumber because they are crunchy, sweet, and equally good eaten fresh or made into any kind of pickles. The round, lemon-shaped cukes come on in just two months, fruiting on long vines that are easy to tie up onto a trellis or stake so the fruit stays clean and accessible.

Lemon cukes have a mild, juicy texture, creamy color, and non-bitter skins. Pick them young before they color up to yellow and get tough. This old variety has been passed along in families for many generations. Try them chopped up with fresh dill and yogurt, or treat yourself to any number of fresh vegetable salads dressed with a sweet-and-sour vinaigrette.

Three essential herbs

Basil Basil adds color and perfume and spicy sweet flavor to most summer vegetables and is the soul-mate of tomatoes. It's easy to grow this tropical heat-lover from seed if you are meticulous about waiting until the soil is warmed and nights and days are consistently above 55° F. Sow seeds and keep beds evenly moist for best results. Thin plants and use the thinnings in your early salads. Pinch the plants when they are about 6 inches tall to encourage branching. Keep stems of garden-harvested leafy basil in a vase of water to keep them fresh in the kitchen. Use basil lavishly; you'll have lots! Purée basil with olive oil and freeze in zip-lock bags to make pesto sauce in the winter—it's best not to add the other ingredients until you actually make the sauce.

Garlic chives This perennial herb is one of my favorite everyday cooking companions. Garlic chives' strappy, flat leaves grow in clumps like regular chives and also produce pretty white edible blossoms. The seed likes a cool, moist place to germinate, but mature plants are very heat-tolerant. Plants form bright green mounds, ready all season to clip for a sweet and very digestible chive-garlic flavor without the fuss or mess of peeling garlic cloves. Try garlic chives freshly chopped onto salads, over tomatoes, onions, potatoes, peppers, or squash, or to season rice, pasta, or noodles.

Italian or "flat leaf" parsley This fine parsley variety has broader, flatter leaves with a milder, sweeter flavor than the curly type. Use it combined with fresh lemon juice if you are cutting back on salt. Freshly snipped parsley is a treat chopped up in any lettuce salad, over tomatoes, cucumbers, or steamed summer squash. The seed germinates slowly but reliably in cool, moist conditions and grows into lovely plants with graceful sprays of shiny, dark green leaves to harvest often and liberally all season. Feed frequently with a high-nitrogen fertilizer to encourage strong growth.

FAVORITE BEAN VARIETIES

Bush beans, green:
 'Derby'
 'Slankette'
 'Provider'
 'Jade'
 'Astrelle'
Bush beans, gold:
 'Roc d'Or'
 'Goldkist'
Bush beans, purple:
 'Purple Teepee'
 'Royal Burgundy'
Pole beans:
 'Fortex'
 'Blue Lake Pole'
 'Emerite'
 'Meralda'

Heirloom Plants for the Kitchen Garden

BY DORIS BICKFORD-SWARTHOUT

OST OF US ARE aware of the need to preserve endangered wild-flowers and wildlife from extinction. Today, because food plants are becoming genetically engineered and many more are hybridized, it is also vital to protect and preserve the biodiversity in what remains of our horticultural heritage. Heritage gardening with heirloom vegetables also adds an exciting extra dimension to the various stages of gardening: planning, planting, cultivating, and harvesting. With a sense of cultural continuity, one can not only re-live history but ultimately taste it!

Heirloom plants can seldom be found in large commercial catalogs or at nurseries. You can find these open-pollinated varieties, which will come true from seed and which date back at least to the 1930s, by searching specialty catalogs (see "Mail-Order Resources," page 104).

Planting, cultivating, and harvesting heirloom vegetables all add an exciting extra dimension to kitchen gardening: With a sense of cultural continuity, you can not only re-live history but ultimately taste it!

The following heirlooms are relatively easy to locate in catalogs of companies specializing in heritage plants. You will also find a few in general catalogs, but they will not always be identified as heirlooms or dated. After you get started with heirloom gardening, you'll have fun tracking down the more elusive varieties. Luckily, there are still a large number to be discovered and savored by contemporary gardeners who want to do their share in preserving genetic diversity in their kitchen gardens.

'Red Brandywine' tomato (1885) Indeterminate vine, deep red color, very productive, wonderful flavor. Probably the most popular of the heirloom tomatoes, the one to which all others are compared. Three others to try: 'Ponderosa' (1891), 'Golden Queen' (1882), and 'Jeff Davis' (1890s). There are probably more heirloom tomatoes available than any other vegetable.

'Bountiful' bush bean (early 19th century) Practically rust- and mildew-proof. Prolific bearer. Thick, broad and long beans. An added bonus: After ripening in the fall, this heirloom makes an excellent shell bean.

'Old Homestead' pole bean (listed in some catalogs as dating from 1891; others, from 1864) Maules' 1892 catalog states that this is an old variety originally sold under the name of 'Kentucky Wonder', which may account for the confusion. Whatever the date, it is a marvelous bean. Enormously productive. Stringless, large, and tender.

'Early Blood' turnip beet (listed in 1870s catalogs as a newer, improved variety) Quite early, smooth, and turnip-shaped. Often passed over in favor of 'Detroit Dark Red' (1892), perhaps because the latter is still quite easy to locate. 'Early Blood' turnip beet, however, is tender and sweet and of very good quality.

'Oxheart' carrot (1880s) Short and very thick. Especially good for heavier soils; easily pulled. Extra good quality. For a longer carrot, 'Danver's Half-Long' (1870s) is smooth, sweet, and tender. This is probably the most popular of the heirloom carrots.

'Early Russian' cucumber (1850) One of the earliest varieties. Small, averaging 3 to 4 inches long. Wonderful flavor for salads or small, crisp pickles. For a larger cucumber, the best choice is 'Long Green Improved' (1870s), a prolific producer from 10 to 12 inches long. It makes super-delicious cucumber sandwiches.

'Simpson's Black-Seeded' lettuce (before 1880) A favorite from the beginning, this lettuce grows large, thin, crisp leaves. Yellowish green in color, it withstands summer heat amazingly well, especially if grown where it has partial shade for half a day. Another fine lettuce is 'Paris White Cos', a romaine type that dates back to at least the 1860s. The pale green leaves are very erect and the quality is lasting.

'Alderman' peas (1878) A tall vine growing from 5 to 6 feet, making for easy picking. The 5-inch-long pods are filled with large peas. In the 1890s, a pea was sold under the name 'Telephone' (named for the marvelous invention that households were beginning to enjoy). Many believe this was 'Alderman' renamed. Some catalogs now use both names when describing the pea.

'Red Heart' sweet pepper (1920s) Dark red and heart-shaped, the sweetest pepper ever grown, according to everyone who tries it. The plants are productive and the fruit medium-sized. Great for stuffing. American-grown sweet peppers from the 19th and early 20th centuries tend to be hard to find. However, many are now being found in Eastern Europe and are said to be superb. One such is 'Golden Summit', a Yugoslavian heirloom that has been grown for over 200 years.

'Cocozelle' summer squash (1920s) A zucchini listed in 1920s catalogs as Italian bush marrow. A compact type producing well in a small space. For something from the mid-1880s, the classic is 'Yellow Crookneck'. Both deserve a place in the kitchen garden.

'Southport Red Globe' onion (1860s) The ground cannot be too rich for onions and must be friable and kept weed free. Onions are one of the few vegetables that can be grown on the same spot every year as long as it is kept well fertilized. The 'Southport White Globe' onion is similar except for color. Both are flavorful and good keepers.

'Cocozelle' is a compact zucchini that produces well in a small space.

'Southport Red Globe' onion is quite flavorful and keeps well.

Compact Vegetables for Small Kitchen Gardens

BY SERLE IAN MOSOFF

IF YOU HAVE ONLY a small space but want to plant a kitchen garden, you can deploy one or several of the following strategies for making your small plot as productive as possible. You can grow varieties that are small versions of full-sized vegetables or grow varieties that are large when mature but can or should be harvested when small. Then there are vegetable types that are inherently small. Finally, there are full-sized vegetables that are so productive they make up for the extra room they take. Your choice of strategy should depend on the location of the kitchen garden and your own tastes. In most cases, the most productive small plot will combine all these strategies.

Say you've found the right space for your kitchen garden, maybe 3 feet by 6

In a small garden you can grow full-sized varieties of open-leafed lettuces, and harvest just the outer leaves. Try 'Red Sails' for its gorgeous burgundy-colored leaves.

feet, just outside the back door near the kitchen. It gets at least a half day of sun. You've added organic material in the form of compost or rotted manure, turned over the ground or maybe even double-dug the area, and you're ready to go. In a small garden, you'll want to plant a little bit of many things. My strategy for a small kitchen garden is to plant greens and avoid most of the fruiting plants because of their size and length of time to harvest, so I skip even my very favorite small Oriental eggplants and peppers (although I've proposed some compact varieties if you simply must have them). However, I'm of the school that believes that a garden without a tomato plant is not a garden, so I will talk about suitable tomatoes.

Greens My favorite green is endive, *Cichorium endivia*. Slightly bitter, its serrated leaves produce an evanescent tingle on the tongue. The finest of the varieties is also the smallest and oldest—'Tres Fine Maraichere'—an old open-pollinated variety from France that matures to a head of single-serving size and is the definition of an elegant French salad. The plant forms a small rosette of finely cut leaves like a small looseleaf lettuce. The center of the plant is creamy yellow, the exterior leaves green. If you want to go the extra step, you can blanch the plant by lifting the outer leaves and tying them around the head about 10 days before harvest. I've successfully used a rubber band; some growers place an upside-down plate over the plant. Once the head is blanched, I cut the stem at ground level, rinse the head under running water, and dry upside down. Serve each head as a single serving, with the rosette spread on a salad plate, drizzled with a mild vinaigrette and sprinkled with a blue cheese. This variety can be planted on 6-inch centers and harvested after 60 days.

Most eggplants like to sprawl, but 'Bambino', a nice mini-eggplant, is only 12 inches tall and adapts well to container-growth.

Lettuces are the backbone of a salad—and of a small kitchen garden. The smallest cos or romaine type is 'Little Gem', also sold as 'Small Density' and 'Sucrine'. This delightful little plant won an award of merit from the Royal Horticultural Society and produces small, elongated heads of sweet, soft leaves. It can be planted on 6-inch centers and harvested after 65 days.

The smallest butterhead is 'Tom Thumb', an heirloom variety. I don't find the flavor to be quite as fine as some of the standard varieties, but it shines in ease of growth and in presentation. Cut the plant at the soil line, wash carefully, and serve each person his or her own individual plant, perhaps surrounded by croutons and drizzled with a balsamic vinaigrette. This variety can be planted on 6-inch centers and harvested after 65 days. An added bonus is that, if harvested as suggested, 'Tom Thumb' will "come again" and provide a second harvest, sprouting from the root you left in the ground.

Open-leafed lettuces are best grown using full-sized varieties and a partial-harvest strategy. As the lettuce grows, begin harvesting just the outer leaves, maintaining the growing plant at a small size and providing yourself with an early harvest. My favorites, not particularly small but suited to partial harvesting, are 'Oak Leaf' for green leaves and 'Red Sails' for red leaves.

A good choice is mesclun, a mixture of lettuces and greens that are meant to be sown together and harvested while the leaves are still young and tender. Sow the mixture in blocks, and harvest one portion of the block at a time by cutting off the leaf tops. Mesclun is a good candidate for "cut and come again" harvesting.

Corn salad (mâche) is a great favorite, too. Sown in fall or early spring for a

If you love beets, grow white and yellow varieties ('Burpee Golden', above, is the best yellow), along with the usual red. Pick beets year-round when they are still small, under 2 inches in diameter.

midspring harvest, corn salad can be block-sown by scattering seed over a 1-foot square, and harvested as soon as the rosettes form. All varieties are small and little differentiated from each other.

Onions In a small garden you can grow members of the genus *Allium*— onions, scallions, chives, shallots, garlic. There seems little reason to grow full-sized globe onions when space is at a premium, but shallots take up little room and are a fine gourmet touch. Garlic requires a long growing season but needs little room.

Onion sets are a great way to get the garden started in spring. Once tall enough, they can be pulled and used as green onions, and the garden space planted with something else. Plant each onion set in spring as early as you can set foot in the garden. Push the sets into the ground about 1 inch apart so the tops are just buried. Harvest as soon as you like and continue harvesting until early summer, when the onions begin to bulb and the leaves toughen.

True scallions, or non-bulbing onions, can be purchased as seeds or as started plants. 'Ishikuro' and 'Iwatsuki' are good choices. Start seeds indoors, and plant out in early spring. You can go the extra step and plant these varieties in a trench 6 inches deep, which you gradually fill in as the plant grows. By covering the plant with soil and excluding light, you will get an elegant 6-inch-long white stalk great for grilling.

Easy to grow, perennial, and with pretty edible flowers are the two chives: *Allium schoenoprasum*, the purple-flowered, delicately onion-flavored type, and *Allium odorum* or Chinese chives, the white-flowered, lightly garlic-flavored variety. Both grow in round clumps of straplike leaves, which can be snipped as needed starting in earliest spring and continuing until hard frost. Cut individual leaves at ground level rather than giving the plant a haircut. Use in dips, on baked potatoes, on meats, and in salads. Use the flowers in salads or as a garnish. Chinese chives can also be lightly stir-fried and eaten as a vegetable. Get plants or seeds from your garden center or a friendly neighbor, or harvest seeds from the flower heads, sow indoors early in the year and plant out after frost 6 inches apart in each direction. Plants can easily be divided at any time but spring is best.

Herbs The small kitchen garden must have herbs. In my estimation, the most useful are oregano and basil. Grow either common oregano, *Origanum vulgare*, or Greek oregano, *Origanum vulgare* spp. *hirtum*, which is more pungent. One plant is enough; buy it at the garden center, and give it 9 inches on all sides.

The other herb that always appears in my garden or on my windowsill, no matter how small, is basil. Grow basil from seed or buy started plants, and stay with the standard variety, *Ocimum basilicum,* for its large leaves and strong flavor. Four to six plants should be sufficient; transplant on 6-inch centers.

I use oregano and basil for flavoring olive oil; add it to the oil with several cloves of peeled garlic, let it stand at room temperature for several days, then strain and store the oil in the refrigerator. One basil plant and six to nine sprigs of oregano provide enough leaves to flavor a quart of oil.

If you have room, by all means buy one rosemary plant and plant it in a 6- to 12-inch container near the garden so you can take it inside in the fall. Rosemary is a tender perennial and very sensitive to lack of water, but if you keep it watered on a sunny windowsill, it will provide you with leaves all winter.

Carrots   There are several delightful small varieties of carrots; each seedsman seems to have a different type. 'Kundulus', ball-shaped and about 1 to 2 inches in diameter at maturity, matures in 62 to 68 days and can be grown in containers. The 1992 All-America winner 'Thumbelina' (64 to 70 days) is a bit larger and widely adapted. 'Little Finger' produces 3- to 4-inch-long cylindrical roots.

Beets   The classic small red beet is 'Spinel' (50-55 days), which should be picked when it is 1 inch in diameter. 'Little Ball' is earlier and widely available. But if you love beets, you must grow white and yellow varieties along with the usual red. The best yellow is 'Burpee Golden', the best white 'Albino Vereduna'. Pick them year-round when they are still small, under 2 inches in diameter.

Tomatoes   Everyone wants tomatoes, even if they only have a windowsill. You can grow tomatoes in tubs or pots. There are "patio" types that actually survive in small pots and produce a fair number of small tomatoes. 'Tiny Tim' and 'Small Fry' hybrids are good varieties. In a pot or a small garden, it is impossible to grow standard tomato plants and achieve 30 to 35 pounds per plant harvest, as can be done in a well-cultivated full-sized plot using intensive growing procedures, but you can still obtain a good harvest by growing one full-sized tomato plant trained against a wall or trellis on the side of the garden where it is least likely to shade the rest of the garden. I prefer the small-fruited indeterminate types 'Gardener's Delight' (open-pollinated) and 'Sweet 100' (hybrid) trained to one or two leaders and trellised. If trellising is too much work, try one of the bush types mentioned above, or the AAS winner 'Patio' hybrid.

Peppers and Eggplants   I'm not sure either peppers or eggplants are really appropriate in a small garden, but if you must, a nice mini-eggplant is 'Bambino', which is only 12 inches tall and can be container-grown. There are few mini-peppers, but 'Park's Pot Hybrid' is a nice 12-inch-tall variety that produces peppers in 45 days and also can be grown in a container.

Cucumbers   Let's face it, cucumbers need room. You can grow a bush variety, especially useful for container growing, but to my taste the especially good-flavored varieties are all Oriental vining types such as 'Suyo Long' or 'Kyoto', which are worth the effort of training up a trellis on the side of the garden. If the thought of trellising doesn't appeal to you, try 'Burpless Bush' (42 days), 'Bush Crop' hybrid (55 days), or 'Pot Luck' (52 days).

Fruits and Edible Flowers for the Kitchen Garden

o kitchen garden would be complete without some fruits to sweeten the harvest and edible flowers to bring elegance and piquancy to summer meals. Here are some recommendations.

Small fruit plants

The following fruit plants require 12 square feet or less per plant; in the right spot, they'll cast less shade onto other sun-loving plants than standard-sized fruit plants. You may have to plant two or more of some of these plants if they are to produce fruit, though; check with your nursery to see which of these fruits are *self-fruitful* (meaning they do not require another plant of the same species to produce fruit) and which are *self-sterile* (meaning they need to be planted with a different variety of the same species to bear fruit). Some of the plants, including the apples, pears, plums, blackberries, raspberries, grapes,

FRUITS		
	SPACING (SQ. FT.)	YIELD (LBS.)
Apple, dwarf	7	60
Apple, semi-dwarf	12	150
Blackberry, erect, semi-erect	5	3
Blackberry, trailing	10	3
Blueberry		
highbush	5	7
lowbush	2	1
rabbiteye	8	15
Currant	6	8
Gooseberry	5	8
Grape	8	15
Juneberry, bushes	6	20
Kiwi	8	150
Pear, dwarf	8	60
Plum	10	75
Raspberry	2	3
Strawberry	1	2

and kiwis, can be trained onto walls or other supports and pruned in ways that will reduce the shade they cast even further—and create an interesting decorative element. The list above was provided by Lee Reich, editor of BBG's *Growing Fruits* (Handbook #147), where you'll find a wealth of information on fruit cultivation.

Edible flowers

Flowers are more than just decorative touches. They can provide flavor and fragrance to a meal as well, or an elegant touch to desserts. Some flowers, such as tulips and zucchini blossoms, are large enough to stuff with chicken or other main-course salads. Use others as flavorings in herbal teas, vinegars, sorbets, custards, butters, soups, and sauces. Fill a bottle of wine vinegar with borage or chive flowers. Use rose water, made by boiling fragrant rose petals in water, as a substitute for vanilla flavoring. Provided they haven't been sprayed with pesticides, the following flowers are edible. The following list was provided by Suzy Bales.

EDIBLE FLOWERS

Apple (*Malus* spp.)

Bee balm (*Monarda* spp.)

Begonia, tuberous (*Begonia* x *tuberhybrida*)

Borage (*Borago officinalis*)

Broccoli (*Brassica oleracea*)

Chives (*Allium schoenoprasum*)

Cornflower (*Centaurea cyanus*)

Daylily (*Hemerocallis* spp.)

Geranium, scented (*Pelargonium* spp.)

Hollyhock (*Alcea rosea*)

Hyssop (*Hyssopus officinalis*)

Jasmine (*Jasminum* spp.)

Johnny-jump-up (*Viola* x *wittrockiana*)

Lilac (*Syringa vulgaris*)

Marigold (*Tagetes* spp.)

Mustard (*Brassica* spp.)

Nasturtium (*Tropaeolum* spp.)

Pansy (*Viola* x *wittrockiana*)

Pea (*Pisum* spp.)—**Not sweet peas, which are poisonous**

Pinks (*Dianthus* spp.)

Plum (*Prunus* spp.)

Pot marigold (*Calendula officinalis*)

Rose (*Rosa* spp.)

Scarlet runner bean (*Phaseolus coccineus*)

Squash (*Cucurbita* spp.)

Strawberry (*Fragaria* spp.)

Thyme (*Thymus* spp.)

Tulip (*Tulipa* spp.)

Violet (*Viola cornuta*)

Kitchen gardeners across the continent must contend with very different kinds of soil, varying amounts of sun and rain per year, and their own worst pests and diseases. Different areas also have different culinary traditions. These variations have led to regional styles of kitchen gardening.

In the pages that follow, veteran kitchen gardeners from the Northeast, Southeast, North and Midwest, Southwest, and Pacific Northwest give you tips on how to prepare your soil, how to cope with climatic extremes, the best plants for your area, and even some suggestions on how to prepare your harvest.

⚔

The Northeast

BY CATHY WILKINSON BARASH

NEW ENGLANDERS are known for their frugal nature, and perhaps that is reflected in the abundance of fruits and vegetables grown in their kitchen gardens. Any thrifty person can appreciate the financial benefit of growing his or her own produce—and, in season, the choices are far greater than those in the local supermarket. Out of season, many thrifty gardeners draw on a stockpile of home-canned, frozen, or otherwise preserved goods from the summer's bounty.

For some Northeasterners, an edible garden is limited by climatic factors. The farther north the garden, the later the last frost date in spring and the earlier the first autumn frost. A gardening friend of mine in the Catskill Mountains (USDA Zones 3 to 4) can usually count on frost-free time only between Memorial Day and Labor Day. My Long Island garden (Zone 7) is generally frost-free from April 20 to October 20.

Other gardeners easily overcome the weather by using season extenders like cold frames and hoop houses. They are able to harvest year-round, even if winter temperatures plunge to -20° F. They can harvest from their cold frames frisée, radicchio, arugula, sorrel, escarole, mizuna, mustard, dandelion, lettuces, chicory, spinach, mâche, and miner's lettuce right through the winter. Add to these marvelous greens the crunch of fresh carrots and radishes and the rich, oniony flavor of leeks, and you have the makings of a great meal.

I take a more middle-of-the-road approach, using some technology and gadgets to extend my growing season. My favorite is the "Wall o' Water" (a cage of plastic tubes that you can fill with water). The warmth that the water absorbs

Dent- or flint-type corns work best for homemade cornmeal, and 'Hopi Blue', left, is a good blue-kerneled flint type.

Beans such as 'Jacob's Cattle' not only taste delicious but also look delectable in glass jars placed (out of direct sunlight) around the kitchen.

from the sun during the day keeps the plants well insulated from night chill, and because its top is open, I don't have to worry about the plants getting too hot in the daytime. As a result, I can put individual tomato plants in the garden in April and have my first harvest in June.

New Englanders grow plants for traditional dishes—beets for red flannel hash; potatoes for chowders (New England clam chowder, fish chowder, corn chowder); corn for the quintessential clam or lobster bake; shelling beans for Boston baked beans; cabbage, carrots, and potatoes for New England boiled dinner—but even among these classic kitchen-garden plants are some new and old favorites.

Beets The standard red beet may be 'Detroit Dark Red' or 'Sangria', but 'Cylindra', with its elongated shape, is the choice for cooks who pickle beets. 'Burpee's Golden' has all the sweet earthy flavor of red beets, but its yellow color doesn't bleed into foods as do red beets. 'Little Ball' is a great small beet, especially good for grilling. The Italian heirloom 'Chioggia' is beautiful with concentric red and white stripes; related to the sugar beet, it is decidedly sweeter than any other beet.

Potatoes Potatoes have long been a New England staple, and Maine has a reputation for the best potatoes—they challenge the dry Idahos any day. Today, gardeners are looking beyond the traditional 'Kennebec' and 'Red Pontiac' to more unusually colored and shaped varieties. 'French Fingerling', 'Ruby Crescent', and 'Russian Banana' all have an elongated shape. 'Yukon Gold' is a favorite yellow-fleshed potato, with 'Bintje' and 'Gold Nugget' running close seconds. Nothing is quite as colorful as a rainbow-hued plate of sliced potatoes. Drizzle with a little olive oil, sprinkle with salt and freshly ground pepper and a dash of rosemary, thyme, or oregano, and you've got a great side dish. 'Lavender' has light lavender skin and flesh. 'Peruvian Blue' is a small potato with deep purple flesh. 'Blaze' lights up the plate with its pink and yellow flesh. 'Cinnabar' is unusual with waxy, deep maroon skin. 'Rojo' is

Use red cabbage, such as 'Red Acre' or 'Ruby Ball' (right), in cole slaw or as the basis for a colorful sauerkraut.

'Cylindra' beets, with their unusual elongated contours, are the choice for cooks who like to pickle beets.

called a pink-fleshed potato, but the color is nearly red. 'Gold Rae' is gorgeous, with rays of pink that radiate through the bright yellow flesh.

Corn One of the best white sweet corns for the Northeast is 'Silver Queen', while 'Early Sunglow' and 'Golden Bantam' are favored yellows, and 'Honey and Pearl' is a great bicolor. It's fun to grow some popcorn—for popping the whole cob in the microwave, or drying for fall decorations. 'Strawberry' bears small ears with red kernels, while 'Miniature Blue' has deep blue kernels. Some cooks like to make their own cornmeal from their harvested corn—dent or flint type corns are best. 'Bloody Butcher' is bold in the garden, growing up to 12 feet tall with red-kerneled ears. 'Hopi Blue' is a good blue-kerneled variety.

Beans Beans come in a wide range of colors; the dried beans are attractive in glass jars placed (out of direct sunlight) around the kitchen. Some of my recommendations include the New England favorite 'Soldier', 'Large Royal Kidney',

With concentric red and white stripes, the Italian heirloom 'Chioggia' is beautiful when sliced. This relative of the sugar beet is decidedly sweeter than any other beet.

Nothing is quite as colorful—or quite as tasty—as a rainbow-hued plate of sliced potatoes.

'Great Northern' (essential for baked beans), 'Jacob's Cattle', 'French Navy', prolific 'Dutch Brown' (also good for baked beans), and 'Black Turtle Soup'.

Cabbage Cabbage varieties, such as the heirloom 'Early Jersey Wakefield' and 'Premium Late Flat Dutch', are fine for a boiled dinner, but even New England palates appreciate some of the other brassicas and their uses. Red cabbage, such as 'Red Acre' and 'Ruby Ball', are great in cole slaw or made into a colorful sauerkraut. Savoy cabbages, including 'Savoy Ace' and 'Savoy King', are perfect for making stuffed cabbage or cabbage soup. And the Oriental varieties—like 'Bok Choy', 'Jade Pagoda', 'Mei Qing Choi', and 'Pak Choy'—round out the garden. Picked small, they are perfect whole in stir-fries or vegetable medleys, and all are easy to grow.

Carrots Many New Englanders complain about the ubiquitous rocks and stones; every spring, it seems, the soil gives birth to more rocks. However, gardeners here persist in growing many root crops. Not only do potatoes and beets grow well in prepared soil, but so do carrots. One trick some gardeners have for loosening the soil is to plant radishes with the carrots. Also, the radishes germinate faster, thus marking the spot where the carrots will eventually emerge. With good mulching in fall (with salt hay or shredded leaves), you can harvest carrots all winter long. Standard sweet carrots include 'Scarlet Wonder', 'Imperator Long', 'Chantenay', 'Scarlet Nantes', 'Royal Chantenay', and 'Danvers Half Long'. For those with the most challenging soil, there are a number of small or round carrots: 'Little Finger', 'Parisier', 'Thumbelina', and 'Short 'n Sweet'.

Peas In my area, it is traditional to plant peas on St. Patrick's Day (March 17), but in three out of the past five years, it has been impossible as the garden has been buried in snow or ice. As soon as it is plantable, however, in go the peas and the pea supports. I prefer sugar snap peas to the old-fashioned shelling pea or snow peas; they can be harvested over a longer time. My favorite varieties include 'Sugar Snap', 'Sugar Ann', and 'Sugar Bon'. I do enjoy a good English pea—especially 'Precovile', 'Lincoln', or the classic 'Laxton's Progress'. 'Novella' is a delight for the multitude of tendrils it produces; it is self-supporting when planted thickly and the tendrils are delicious served raw in salads or in a vegetable stir-fry.

Greens Every kitchen garden has its share of greens, which are among the first crops of the gardening season. I sow mesclun mix in containers at the end of my driveway and create a 6-inch border of colorful mixed greens to edge my garden. I am partial to red looseleaf lettuces such as 'Juliet', 'Lollo Rosso', 'Red Sails', 'Sangria', 'Red Deer Tongue', 'Red Oakleaf', and 'Red Salad Bowl'. 'Merveille de Quatre Saisons' is slow to bolt and often makes it through the summer intact as I continue to harvest outer leaves. Mâche, or corn salad, is particularly lovely as an edging with its dark green rosettes of leaves. I make successive sowings of arugula every two weeks.

Tomatoes Tomatoes are the quintessential kitchen garden plants. I try to grow as many as I can fit in; often I end up with tomatoes in containers gracing the end of the driveway. Gardeners in more northerly areas may need to grow determinate varieties, such as 'Subarctic Plenty', 'Ole', 'Earlirouge', or 'Sub Arctic Maxi', but some of the more prolific (and flavorful) indeterminate tomatoes are worth trying, including 'Sweet Chelsea', 'Early Cascade', 'Early Girl', and especially the abundant 'Sweet 100' cherry tomato. What's really exciting are all the unusual varieties—tomatoes in rainbow hues. In my book, golden-orange 'Sungold' and yellow 'Taxi' can beat out any other tomato for flavor out of hand—and they're beautiful additions to any dish. Other tasty unusual tomatoes are 'Olympic Flame', 'Evergreen' (green when ripe), tiny 'Yellow Currant', green-shouldered 'Purple Cherokee', striped 'Pineapple Tomato' or 'Mr. Stripey', 'Golden Queen', and 'White Beauty'.

The Southeast

BY CYNTHIA HIZER

T'S THE SECOND WEEK in February, and I'm up to my boot tops in garden chores. Five varieties of potatoes are waiting to go into my Georgia kitchen garden this week, along with Vidalia (granex) onion plants, "multiplying" onions, leeks, carrots, beets, English peas, turnip greens, rape (sometimes called rapini), Bibb lettuce, and early flowers. The roses have been pruned, the rosemary bushes moved.

That's gardening here in the Southeast. With nary a month's rest, we are gardening hard until Thanksgiving, still digging things in December, and starting seeds in January. The South is a great place to garden, if you *really* like to garden.

Southeastern traditions

The South has a reputation for being "fragrant," and you can see why: We are in bloom virtually every month. In March, the peaches blossom. In December, camellias. The low-lying haze and humidity hold the wonderful scents close to the earth, at nose level. It is a constant parade of smells and beauty that draws us to the garden.

In this land of magnolia-scented nights and stubborn traditions, we hold dear to our hearts the classic English garden. The English and the Scots were the first to land on Southern shores, so our kitchen gardens, like our cuisine and architecture, were based on the English style. We still like picket fences and gardens shaped in squares. Cottage flowers abound.

The cuisine didn't stay English for long—a hybrid cuisine was quickly born. Thomas Jefferson's famous garden and table at Monticello in Virginia were

In the Southeast, a hybrid cuisine includes okra (above) from Africa, peas from England, and tomatoes and hot peppers from the West Indies.

Southern gardeners enjoy the sweet scents of camellias and the fiery taste of hot peppers.

among the first to showcase English, Native American, and African ingredients together (see "A Traditional American Kitchen Garden," page 8).

Our gardens still do: shallots and peas from England; watermelons, sweet potatoes, collard greens, and okra from Africa; tomatoes and hot peppers from the West Indies; and native onions, squash, pumpkins, and beans all thrive side-by-side in our gardens and our cooking. Vegetable dishes have always been a highlight of Southern cooking, and, today, that same tradition continues, always with an added dash of something hot.

Pitfalls of gardening in the Southeast

Our biggest shortcoming is the very thing that also makes our gardens so lush: lots of heat and humidity. Our climate causes organic matter to burn off quickly, so we must replenish the soil annually with plenty of compost and manure. The mostly acidic soil needs regular applications of lime, too, usually on an annual basis. Phosphorus can be found, but it is deep below the soil surface.

To bring it up, we plant deep-rooted rye in the winter and buckwheat in the summer. The roots of these grains absorb the phosphorus, and when we turn them under to decompose, they release this nutrient to fruiting plants such as tomatoes and peppers, as well as flowers.

Because we require so much of our gardens, the soil has to do double and triple duty. While gardeners in the North are just gearing up for their first planting, Southerners have already harvested once, are planting a second round, and planning the third. This takes a lot out of the soil, which already needs help to begin with. We must be sure to give back to the soil as much as it gives to us, month in and month out.

We also have to be prepared for bugs and weeds before they arrive. I weed early and often to keep ahead of things. It's best to search out insect pests in the larval stage, when it doesn't take a chemical arsenal to control them. Organic pest controls are best. Sprinkle diatomaceous earth on potatoes, radishes, and eggplants to get the potato beetle larvae and flea beetles; Bt (*Bacillus thuringiensis berliner*) on cabbage family members (brassicas) to remove cabbage loopers; and summer oil on roses and fruit trees to get rid of their common pests. A plant-derived pesticide, neem oil usually vanquishes the toughest pest of all—the Japanese beetle. If neem doesn't work, we reluctantly resort to another botanical insecticide, rotenone. Rotenone will get the beetles, but it will take beneficial insects down with them, so we avoid it when possible.

Finally, our plants are prone to fungal diseases due, once again, to the extreme heat and humidity. Therefore, when planning a kitchen garden, it's important to give the plants plenty of room for good air circulation.

What grows best

The South has not only a long growing season, but also gentle weather and rain when it is needed. Together, these climatic conditions make the region perfect for growing a wide variety of garden treasures, especially such heat-lovers as beans, tomatoes, okra, sweet potatoes, and peanuts. Our soil produces a soft, low-protein wheat, crucial to the delicate biscuits and pie crusts for which the area is famous. Southern grapes, called muscadines, are sweeter than northern ones. Sweet vidalia onions grow in the sulfur-deficient soil of southeastern Georgia. Upland mountains yield rich-tasting tomatoes and white corn.

With at least 10 months of garden activity, the Southeastern kitchen garden is best situated for easy access. Since we get a lot of use out of our patios, we often

Native American pumpkins (above), onions, squash, and beans thrive in Southern gardens and cooking.

plant our kitchen garden nearby if possible. However, the hot afternoon sun can be very damaging, so the garden should be planted where it can get a few hours of protective shade in mid-afternoon.

The heat is always an issue, and we take care to choose varieties that thrive in hot weather. If we grow 'Alaska' peas, we plant them in February, not April. And tomatoes that continue to set bloom at 90° F. earn high marks. Fall gardens are often our best: The pests have gone, but the weather is still balmy. We may give up on tomatoes in the heat of August, but by September, with the return of cooler temperatures, we are back in the mood to care for the plants. Greens, potatoes, and summer squash can thrive, often past Thanksgiving. Here are some things we look for:

- Varieties of lettuce that don't bolt (go to seed) quickly in the heat.
- Short-season potatoes. My personal favorite is the 55-day 'Yukon Gold'. (In another life, another location, I will grow 'Russian Banana', but not in Georgia.)
- Early sweet corn. The corn earworms get nasty by July, and we like to have our corn harvested by then.
- Southern peas are great heat-lovers, and have developed a cult following. We have black-eyed peas, yellow-eyed peas, pink-eyed peas, zipper peas, purple crowders, Mississippi silver peas, lady peas, 'White Acre' peas, and dozens of others. They grow easily with a minimum of nitrogen, and offer a healthy vegetable source of protein.

The North and Midwest

BY JENNIFER BENNETT

UST TWO WORDS will almost ensure success in northern and midwestern kitchen gardens: *think frost.* In my USDA Hardiness Zone 4 garden in Ontario, Canada, frost and its constant companion, cold, define what I can grow and when I can grow it. My last spring frost comes around mid-May, and the first fall frost around mid-September. Those are averages. I've also had frost in June and at the end of August. Sometimes, too, the frost-free season can be a full two months longer than I'd expect. Even so, those extra weeks are apt to be cool, especially in spring.

When the soil is 41° F. or colder, vegetable seeds are likely to rot before they

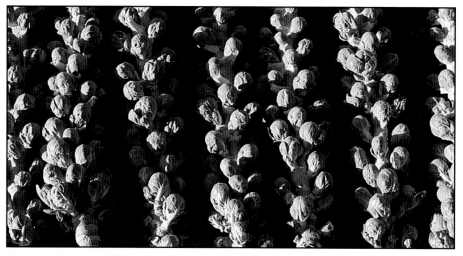

Frost hardy vegetables like Brussels sprouts do better in cool weather than in high heat, and can be direct-sown into the garden.

FROST-HARDY VEGETABLES

Artichokes, Jerusalem
Asparagus
Beans, broad (favas)
Broccoli
Brussels sprouts
Cabbage
Carrots
Chicory
Kale
Onions
Parsley
Parsnips
Peas
Radishes
Rutabaga (winter turnip)
Spinach
Swiss chard

can germinate, and even the hardiest transplants just sit, easy prey for insects and diseases. Not until the soil warms above 41° F. will cold-tolerant plants like peas and spinach grow. The soil has to be much warmer—50° to 55° F.—for frost-tender vegetables to grow. Much can be lost by planting too early, unless certain precautions are taken.

If the frost and cold are against low-zone gardeners in spring, the sun is with us in summer. By the end of June, the sun rises at about 4 am and doesn't set until after 10 pm. Farther north, the days are even longer. The long, hot days of summer mean rapid plant growth, so provided we pay attention to the seasonal brackets that are the frost dates, we can grow just about anything—even watermelons, bell peppers, eggplants, and the biggest beefsteak tomatoes. I choose cultivars carefully, however, looking for those that can be started ahead indoors or purchased as transplants and that will mature rapidly once they are in the garden.

Days-to-maturity listings are important. This number, which signifies the time from outdoor planting to first harvest, is usually listed in seed catalogs or on seed packets. For example, I can pick a big crop of just about any variety of tomato in early September, but if I want ripe tomatoes in July, I'll have to look for a variety that takes 60 days from outdoor transplanting. If I want to grow watermelons, I'll choose a small-fruited type like 'Sugar Baby'.

Variety choice is especially important with frost-tender plants like tomatoes and watermelons. Any cold-zone gardener soon learns to divide all plants into two main groups: frost-tender and frost-hardy, with a few others falling somewhere in between. No kitchen garden is complete without a few frost-tender vegetables, but an untimely frost, especially while the gardener is away on vacation and can't protect the plants, can wipe out the crop. The frost-hardy vegetables, on the other hand, are so reliable that northern pioneers bet their winter survival upon them.

Frost-hardy vegetables

Sow or transplant frost-hardy vegetables into the garden one to four
weeks before the average last spring
frost date. Short periods of cold weather will slow or stop their growth but
won't kill them. Indeed, all of them do
better in cool weather than in high
heat. All the plants listed in the box on
page 90 can be direct-sown into the
garden. Most can also be grown from transplants, although if the plants are set
out too early, growth will be slowed. Peas and root crops do not transplant well,
so they should always be sown directly in the garden. Onions must be grown
from sets or from transplants started at least six weeks ahead indoors. Asparagus and Jerusalem artichokes are perennials that should be given a permanent
spot in the garden.

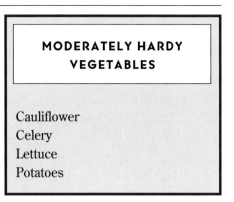

MODERATELY HARDY VEGETABLES

Cauliflower
Celery
Lettuce
Potatoes

Moderately hardy vegetables

Cauliflower, celery, lettuce, and potatoes fall into this category. Direct-sow or
transplant cauliflower and lettuce into the garden anytime from a week before
the average last spring frost date until a week after the frost date. Celery should
be grown from transplants. The foliage of potatoes, which are grown from seed
potatoes (chunks of potato including at least one eye), will be damaged by frost,
but the tubers will survive. Celery and lettuce can take light frost, but will be set
back or killed by longer exposures.

Frost-tender vegetables

Frost-tender vegetables (see the list on page 92) will be harmed or killed by even
a light frost of 29° to 32° F. Unless they are covered by glass or plastic, they
should not go into the garden until after the last average spring frost date. If
there is a frost warning, cover them in the evening, using blankets, weighted
newspapers, buckets, or jars, and do not remove the covers until the temperature is above freezing.

Cultivar choice is especially important with tender plants, because the harvest
should take place before the steady cold weather of fall. Check with seed compa-

---

FROST-TENDER VEGETABLES

Beans, all types except favas
Corn
Cucumbers
Okra
Peppers, all kinds
Potatoes, sweet; yams
Pumpkins
Squash, summer and winter
Tomatoes

nies located in cold regions, or ones that specialize in short-season crops for suitable varieties.

Direct-sow beans and corn. Grow eggplants, gourds, melons, okra, peppers, sweet potatoes, and tomatoes from transplants. Cucumbers, pumpkins, and squash can be either direct-sown or grown from transplants.

Season-extending techniques

To beat frost and cold soil, you not only have to choose the right vegetable and variety and plant it at the right time, but use certain techniques to extend the season and protect the plants.

Plastic mulch A clear polyethylene mulch can raise the soil temperature on a sunny day by about 12° F. This type of mulch is used for tender crops only—the others do better in cool soil. Clear mulch has been proved to hasten the maturity of cucumbers, melons, peppers, tomatoes, and sweet potatoes. Put down the mulch about two weeks earlier than the usual planting date. Then, at planting time, cut an X in the mulch where you want a transplant to go. A black plastic mulch can also be used; it does not raise the soil temperature as well but is better at smothering weeds. Both types of mulch help retain moisture in the soil.

Crop covers As mentioned above, tender crops must be covered in an emergency if there is a frost warning. But crop covers can also be used in a more systematic way. Polyethylene row covers, slit to prevent too much heat buildup, can allow tomatoes and other tender plants to go into the garden as early as a month before the average last spring frost date. Glass or fiberglass are other options. Individual plant covers, such as plastic tepees and clear plastic rings insulated with water, have a similar effect and are a better choice than row covers if you are growing only a few plants.

Cold frames A cold frame is a miniature greenhouse (usually built of wood) about a foot high with a clear plastic or glass roof that slopes toward the south. The cover can be removed on hot days or lifted a bit to allow ventilation. Hardy plants can be grown here from seed, nurtured to transplanting size, and hardened off with the cover removed before they go into the garden. Tender crops, too, can be sown or hardened off in the cold frame, but you'll need to insulate the frame on frosty nights by covering it with a blanket. In Zone 6 and warmer areas, it is possible to overwinter space-efficient frost-hardy plants, especially salad greens, in a cold frame.

Taking advantage of sunlight Where the season is short, the kitchen garden needs as much sun as possible. Taller plants such as asparagus, sunflowers, sweet corn, and staked tomatoes should go at the back—the northern end—so they do not shade other plants.

Containers The soil in containers warms up and cools down faster than the soil in the garden. Tender plants grown in containers placed in the sun will benefit from the extra heat, and can be easily moved under cover in cold weather. Containers can also be moved during the day to follow the sun. Variety choice is important; look for compact varieties recommended for containers or small gardens.

Frost-hardy vegetables such as broccoli ('Romanesco', above) are so reliable that pioneers bet their survival on them.

Windproofing Wind at any time of the year can be damaging, but especially so in cold weather. Consider a windbreak of shrubs such as pea tree (*Caragana pygmaea*) or upright junipers (*Juniperus* species) on the windward side of the garden. Dense annuals such as kochia (*Bassia scoparia,* although this is considered invasive on the Canadian prairies and is prohibited there) or small sunflowers such as 'Sunspot' can create a temporary windbreak. The taller the windbreak, the farther from the garden it must be to prevent root competition and shading.

Raised beds Raised beds in a kitchen garden not only look attractive and make tending the plants easier, but also help warm the soil, since cold air sinks downward and the soil is exposed to solar heat on three sides. Raised beds also provide good drainage, which ensures that early crops do not sit and rot in cold, sodden ground. In a raised bed, incorporate compost, leaf mold, and other forms of organic matter, which help soil drainage and retain warmth, insulating roots against variations in temperature.

The Southwest

BY JANIE MALLOY

A S SOON AS THE GROUND HAS THAWED...”—how many times have we read this? As a garden designer and landscape contractor in Pasadena, California, I spend a lot of time convincing my clients to forget about this and other gardening instructions, because they are inevitably associated with the “norm.” We are not the norm, but the exception. Our summer is not three or four months long; our winter is. And our winter kitchen gardens are as lush, beautiful, fulfilling, and productive as our summer gardens.

Perhaps the only drawback to gardening year-round is the lack of down time. I am busy planning, planting, harvesting, or preserving every month of the year. Sometimes I wish there were entire months when I could curl up by a fire on snowy afternoons and read Jamaica Kincaid or M.F.K. Fisher and daydream about gardening. But most of the time, I feel guilty pleasure while harvesting a fresh salad in the middle of January, wondering how people in colder areas survive without the therapy of gardening.

Winter

In my part of the Southwest, winter is the rainy season and runs from January to March. Cold days dip into the 50°s, but the average temperatures linger in the 60°s. This is the time of year when we harvest, succession sow, prune dormant fruit trees, and plant bare root. We gather fresh tea herbs from the garden and select summer seeds from catalogs. On rainy days, we clean and sharpen our tools in the shed, and eat the fresh kumquats, blood oranges, and pomelos that ripen at this time of year.

In the Southwest, gardeners are busy with their gardens—planning, preparing the soil, planting, harvesting, or preserving—every month of the year.

The transition from winter to spring usually happens during the latter half of March. The slight possibility of a freeze is over by then, and everyone is anxious to plant tomatoes. Every year I beg, scold, and beseech my clients and students not to plant tomatoes in early March. "But the weather is so beautiful," they say. "Yes, but tomatoes are daylight-sensitive," I warn. "You will not get tomatoes much sooner, and it could diminish your total harvest. Lots of big leafy plants, itty-bitty harvest." I find a compromise works best, and suggest they plant early varieties or daylight-neutral tomatoes if they must get a jump on things. March is a splendid time to plant quick-growing cool-weather crops like lettuce and spinach—things that can come out of the garden in May. Carrots should be planted early, for they will develop a tinny taste during the high heat of summer.

Don't plant true heat-lovers like melons (above, 'Moon and Stars') too early in the spring, because they won't take off till summer; plant short-season crops instead.

Spring

Spring unfurls in April and May. I like to plant my tomatoes on or near April Fool's Day; it is my silly tradition. There is also lots of harvesting to do, what with potatoes coming out of the ground and peas waiting to be picked from the trellis. Many short-season crops or varieties that are developed to germinate under cool conditions (like 'Early Sunglow' corn) can be planted early. True heat-lovers, like eggplants, chiles, peppers, and melons, seldom grow quickly if planted too early, and tend to take up space without performing.

Crop rotation means more than moving varieties to alternating locations to build soil and evade insects; in mild-winter climates like ours, crop rotation includes succession sowing. While planning crop rotation, a gardener must consider increasing his or her yield by planting something that can be harvested in time to plant another crop immediately after it—and another after that. Planting year-round requires a gardener to develop a planting rhythm. This is the challenge and the fun of being a gardener in such a marvelous climate. The most important thing is to add compost before planting—every time—because you must feed your soil so your soil can feed your plants.

In the often stifling heat of August and September, peppers and chiles thrive while less hardy plants like tomatoes drop their blossoms.

Summer

Here in Pasadena, summer begins in June but lasts through November. By June, the plants that prefer cooler conditions, like spinach, will have to come out. Keeping lettuce going, to enjoy in a salad with tomatoes, is tricky. We plant heat-tolerant varieties, and try to keep the crop in a cool or shady spot. Starting seeds indoors, and transplanting them outside when they can better handle the high heat, is another technique for extending the harvest. It's ironic that northerners start seeds indoors because it is too cold outside, and we do it because it is too hot.

During August and September, the heat can become stifling, and while the tomatoes are dropping their blossoms, the peppers and chiles are looking content. Unfortunately, tomatoes will drop their blossoms once the temperatures

Eggplant, another heat-lover, takes off during the long summer days of the Southwest.

climb consistently into the 90°s, so if there is a freak heat wave in May or June, then the harvest will be diminished. But all of those tomato flowers that were pollinated during May, June, and July are starting to produce fruit by August. The latter half of August is the time I plant tomatoes for fall harvest. By the time the heat dissipates in October and November, the blossoms are getting pollinated and producing fruit well into December. I know people who overwinter their tomatoes, but I'm not a big fan of turning hardworking annuals into perennials, particularly if they do not do it gracefully.

September is still very hot, and the harvest is in full gear: melons, peppers, eggplants, tomatoes, cucumbers, beans. And of course it's time to start planting some cool-weather crops like Brussels sprouts, cauliflower, cabbage, and broccoli. We can succession-sow these beauties through February. October is the last month of heat for us, and we wrap up the summer harvest with pumpkins for Halloween.

Fall

Both October and November are the best planting months for edible fall crops, but also for ornamental trees and perennials. Not only do we plant the aforementioned cole crops, but also a multitude of greens, peas, and plentiful root crops like carrots, turnips, beets, and parsnips. And, of course, it wouldn't be autumn without planting potatoes, onions, and garlic. December is often the unpredictable month; one year I had sunflowers blooming, and another brought freezing temperatures. I prefer to have as much planting as possible out of the way before mid December, anyway, because it gives me much more time to enjoy the winter holidays.

The Pacific Northwest

BY JAMES R. BAGGETT

MOST OF THE Pacific Northwest's population lives west of the Cascade Mountains, so that's where you'll find most of the region's kitchen gardens. In Oregon, this area includes a narrow coastal strip and a larger inland valley, and in Washington, the coastal strip, a narrower inland valley in the south, and the large Puget Sound area in the north. Climatic variations are mostly related to the proximity to or distance from the Pacific Ocean.

With its long growing season—about 200 days—generally cool summer, and usually mild winter, the area is favored by less drastic extremes than many other areas of North America. This friendly environment for gardening, though,

'Cascadia' and other pea varieties resistant to pea enation mosaic virus grow happily in the Northwest.

is affected by both a marine air flow from the Southwest and a continental air flow from the Northeast, so summers alternate between cool and hot, with temperatures up to 100° F., often with stressful winds. Summers are generally dry, making irrigation a necessary chore. Typical winter weather is mild and damp, but can sometimes be dry and occasionally as cold as 0° F.

Kitchen-garden planning is seriously affected by weather. While temperatures are favorable for planting cool-season or protected warm-season crops as early as April 1, spring rains may prevent normal tillage and planting until June. Raised beds filled with light soil mixes make planting possible, while open gardens are still growing weeds and grass until they can be mowed and tilled. Raised beds also facilitate some winter culture of vegetables and the winter harvest of root crops.

Barring weather problems, May is the prime month for planting; there is little danger of frost by this time, and long-season crops such as squashes mature well when planted in May, except in coastal areas. Tomatoes, peppers, and other warm-season crops normally need no protection if planted after about May 10.

What grows best

Vegetables The Pacific Northwest is a good place to grow all cool-season vegetables and herbs, although not necessarily in midsummer. Peas, especially edible pod (snow peas) and snap peas, are favorites and can be planted from February through July. Avoid planting in late May and June because problems may arise due to hot weather and disease. Be sure to plant pea varieties resistant to pea enation mosaic virus. Oregon State University (OSU) has developed resistant snow peas ('Oregon Sugarpod II' and 'Oregon Giant'), snap peas ('Cascadia'), and shelling peas ('Oregon Trail' and 'Oregon Pioneer'). The variety 'Little

The Northwest has a long growing season—about 200 days—and is favored by less drastic extremes than many other areas. Summer squashes thrive here, as elsewhere.

Marvel' is usually devastated by virus and should not be planted here.

All of the cruciferous vegetables (cole crops and root crops such as radishes and turnips) thrive, but this region has its share of the root maggots, aphids, and worms that plague these crops. Carrots and parsnips thrive and can be harvested through the winter, but winter digging is difficult, and carrots tend to crack and rot unless raised beds are used. Carrots may need cover, such as a mulch, when winter freezes are severe.

Lettuce grows well all season in cooler areas, and slow-bolting varieties are acceptable for summer culture in all parts of the Pacific Northwest. The slow-bolting butterhead variety 'Buttercrunch' is a favorite here. The crisphead lettuce 'Summertime' was developed at OSU for summer conditions, and the older

Northwesterners should plant tomato varieties such as 'Early Girl' (above) that ripen in short order, or they're bound to have a "green tomato" year.

variety 'Ithaca' also is non-bolting and slow to become bitter.

Northwesterners don't grow greens as much as salad crops (mainly leaf and butterhead lettuces), and few people grow the cruciferous greens—turnip greens and collards—that are popular in the South. Spinach doesn't do well in the Pacific Northwest, possibly because the soil pH is too low, but beets, especially sugar beets, make good greens and are much more adaptable than spinach. Sugar beets can be cut for greens several times during the season.

The warm-season crops really define the climatic differences within the Pacific Northwest. Varieties that are adapted to the warmer Willamette Valley of Oregon may not mature at all in the Puget Sound area and along the coast. 'Jubilee', a popular sweet corn variety in the Willamette Valley, will mature when planted as late as July 1, so gardeners can make at least eight weekly plantings in a good season. But 'Jubilee' will not mature in Puget Sound areas such as Mount Vernon, Washington; gardeners in this area must grow the earliest varieties available. Kitchen gardeners in the Willamette Valley and similar areas of Oregon and Washington can grow all warm-season vegetables successfully except for okra and peanuts, and with some extra effort sweet potatoes can be grown but are not very productive. Plant only early varieties of eggplant, preferably in a warm location, and consider using a plastic mulch.

As in every other part of the country, tomatoes may be the most popular vegetable here. All varieties can be grown in the warmer areas of the region, depending on local conditions such as amount of sun. "Green tomato" years will come around often unless you plant early determinate varieties, or certain early indeterminate varieties such as 'Early Girl'. Seedless (parthenocarpic) varieties with large fruits, such as 'Oregon Spring' and 'Siletz', do well here and in other cool or short-season parts of North America because they set early, concentrated crops of fruits when temperatures are too low for normal fruit set. These varieties are highly adapted to early spring culture in cool plastic greenhouses and tunnels, and to normal mid-May, unprotected plantings. In warmer areas, plant later, indeterminate varieties as well, such as 'Big Beef' and 'Better Boy', to sustain production later into the fall. Tomatoes are best grown with drip irrigation to reduce the amount of water that gets on the foliage, which encourages development of diseases. Early blight (*Alternaria*) and late blight (*Phytophthora*) often defoliate tomato plants if the weather is damp in late summer.

Peppers will also succeed here, although they are much more demanding than tomatoes and do poorly or fail in the cooler areas. Squashes and pumpkins are easy to mature and basically trouble-free in the warmer areas, difficult in the cooler areas. Summer squashes thrive as they do elsewhere. Watermelons and muskmelons are marginal. Even in the warmer Willamette Valley, it's hard to consistently grow a good quality melon; your efforts are better spent elsewhere.

Finally, green beans can be grown with ease in most parts of the Northwest. Gardeners here favor Blue Lake types such as the pole 'Blue Lake' or the bush variety 'Oregon 91G'. Beans are mostly trouble-free, but the 12-spot cucumber beetle and mold diseases can be problems.

Herbs Herbs are popular with many gardeners in the Pacific Northwest and are mostly easy to grow, but plantings of perennial herbs and vegetables such as asparagus and rhubarb tend to get overgrown with grass during our mild wet winters. Growing them in raised beds or other closely tended beds is required.

Fruits Where space permits, fruits do well here. Highbush blueberries, which are compact, non-spreading, and attractive, are widely grown and probably the best fruit crop for small gardens in all Northwest areas. Strawberries are also popular and easy to grow, but are susceptible to birds and slugs. Blackberries and raspberries thrive, but tend to sprawl. Gardeners with lots of space can grow fruit trees but, except for pears, they will need much spraying to remain healthy. Avoid peaches because peach leaf curl disease usually destroys the trees, even when a burdensome spray program is followed.

W. Atlee Burpee Co.
300 Park Ave.
Warminster, PA 18991
215-674-9633
215-674-4915
(vegetables, flowers, herbs, and fruits)

The Cook's Garden
P.O. Box 535
Londonderry, VT 05148
802-824-3400
(a wide range of unusual vegetables, flowers, and herbs, including many heirlooms)

Thomas Jefferson Center for Historic Plants
Monticello
P.O. Box 316
Charlottesville, VA 22902-0316
804-984-9860
(seeds harvested from the Monticello gardens, including those grown by Jefferson)

Johnny's Selected Seeds
299 Foss Hill Rd.
Albion, ME 04910
207-437-9297
(annual and perennial flowering plants and grasses)

Landis Valley Museum
2451 Kissel Hill Rd.
Lancaster, PA 17601
717-569-0401 ext 202
(heirloom vegetables, herbs, and fruits with an emphasis on PA German crops)

Native Seeds/Search
2509 North Campbell Ave. #325
Tucson, AZ 85719
520-327-9123
(seeds from crops traditionally grown by native peoples in the Southwest and Mexico)

Nichols Garden Nursery
1190 N. Pacific Hwy.
Albany, OR 97321
503-928-9280
(herbs and unusual vegetables)

Geo. W. Park Seed Co., Inc.
1 Parkton Ave.
Greenwood, SC 29647-0001
800-845-3369
864-223-7333
(flowers, vegetables, herbs, and fruits)

Pepper Gal
P.O. Box 23006
Ft. Lauderdale, FL 33307
954-537-5540
(big selection of hot and sweet peppers)

Pinetree Garden Seeds
Box 300
New Gloucester, ME 04260
207-926-3400
(untreated vegetable, herb, and flower seeds)

Seeds Blüm
Idaho City Stage
Boise, ID 83706
208-342-0858
(heirloom vegetables, herbs, flowers, and seed collections)

Seeds of Change
P.O. Box 15700
Santa Fe, NM 87506-5700
888-762-7333

505-438-8080

(large assortment of organically produced seeds from vegetables, flowers, and herbs, including many heirlooms, and gardening supplies)

Santa Barbara Heirloom Seedling Nursery
P.O. Box 4235
Santa Barbara, CA 93140
805-968-5444
(organically produced heirloom vegetable seedlings)

Seed Savers Exchange
3076 North Winn Rd.
Decorah, IA 52101
319-382-5872
(heirloom vegetables, herbs, fruits, and flowers; available to members of SSE)

Shepherd's Garden Seeds
30 Irene Street
Torrington, CT 06790
203-482-3638
(wide range of flowers, vegetables, and herbs, including many heirlooms)

Territorial Seed Company
P.O. Box 157
Cottage Grove, OR 97424
541-942-9547
(hybrid, open-pollinated, and heirloom vegetables, flowers, and cover crops)

Tomato Growers Supply Co.
P.O. Box 2237
Fort Myers, FL 33902
941-768-1119
(more than 300 tomato varieties including heirlooms, as well as 120-plus varieties of peppers)

CONTRIBUTORS

Carole Turner is the former editor of *Fine Gardening* magazine and the former managing editor of *American Nurseryman* magazine. She is the author of *The Gardener's Guide to Saving Seeds* and a contributor to the Brooklyn Botanic Garden's *Gardener's Desk Reference*. Her own cutting/kitchen garden is in Ridgefield, Connecticut.

Peter J. Hatch is Director of Gardens and Grounds for the Thomas Jefferson Memorial Foundation in Charlottesville, Virginia. He is responsible for the maintenance, interpretation, and restoration of the landscape at Monticello and oversees the educational programs and tours. Hatch is editor of *Thomas Jefferson's Flower Garden at Monticello* and the author of *The Gardens of Monticello* (1992), from which his piece here is adapted.

John D. Simpson is a landscape architect who has designed gardens and parks in the Pacific Northwest and Hawaii for 20 years. He is the author of several articles on garden style, has taught at the University of Oregon Department of Landscape Architecture, and is Director of Parks and Development in Bend, Oregon.

Louisa Jones is a Canadian-born writer who has lived and gardened in Provence, France, since 1975. She is the author of *Gardens of Provence; Provence: A Country Almanac; Art of French Vegetable Gardening,* and *The World of French Vegetable Gardens.*

Suzy Bales is a garden writer, lecturer, photographer, and consultant. She is the author of seven books in the Burpee American Gardening Series, as well as *Ready, Set, Grow* and *Gifts From Your Garden.* Bales created Burpee's line of Designed Gardens seed mixes. She has tended her New York garden for 16 years.

Dayna S. Lane is a professional gardener, writer, lecturer, and photographer. Until moving to Baltimore, Maryland, Dayna was the weekly garden columnist for California's *Santa Cruz County Sentinel Newspaper.* She now writes "From the Ground Up," a monthly column for *Food & Wine's Edible Garden* newsletter.

Robert Kourik is an author, publisher, and consultant dealing in organic, edible, and ornamental landscape care, graywater use, and drip irrigation. He lives in Santa Rosa, California and works with clients throughout the state and the U.S.

Doc and Katy Abraham are lifelong horticulturists who co-host a gardening radio program and write a syndicated gardening column, "The Green Thumb." They have authored several books and numerous magazine articles on gardening, and live and garden in Naples, New York.

Lucy Apthorp Leske, a gardener, writer, and educational consultant, lives on Nantucket Island, Massachusetts, where she writes a weekly column, "Gardening by the Sea," for the *Nantucket Inquirer and Mirror.* Her chapter on indoor kitchen gardening is adapted from an article for *Kitchen Garden* magazine (No. 5), "Windowsill Greens Freshen Up Winter Salads."

Renee Shepherd, a pioneer in popularizing heirloom plants for the kitchen garden, recently started up a new heirloom seed company, Renee's Garden, to supply nurseries; she is also the founder of Shepherd's Garden Seed. With cooking partner Fran Raboff, Shepherd has written two cookbooks for gardening cooks. She lives in Felton, California.

Doris Bickford-Swarthout, an authority on 19th and early 20th century America, is author of *An Age of Flowers: Sense and Sentiment in Victorian America* and *Mary Hallock Foote: Pioneer Woman Illustrator* and of many articles on early country life. She co-owns a bookstore and grows heirloom fruits, flowers, and vegetables in upstate New York.

Serle Ian Mosoff is the founder of The Urban Farmer, Inc., a Port Chester, New York mail-order source for imported vegetable seeds. He writes and lectures on vegetable growing, and is a director of the Westchester and Fairfield Horticultural Society.

Cathy Wilkinson Barash, a lifelong organic kitchen gardener, is the author and photographer of six books, including *Edible Flowers from Garden to Palate*, *The Cultivated Gardener* and *Vines & Climbers*. She is the editor of *Food & Wine*'s *Edible Garden* newsletter. Until recently she lived and gardened in Cold Spring Harbor, New York; she now lives in Iowa.

Cynthia Hizer is a weekly columnist for the *Atlanta Journal and Constitution*, writing on produce, vegetarian cooking, gardening, and agriculture. She owns and runs Hazelbrand, an organic farm in Covington, Georgia, specializing in vegetables and year-round growing.

Jennifer Bennett has been gardening in Ontario, Canada, for 20 years and has won numerous journalism awards, including the Garden Writers Association of America Quill & Trowel award. Her latest book is *The New Northern Gardener* (Firefly, 1996). She writes a monthly gardening column for *Canadian Living*.

Janie Malloy is a landscape contractor and owner of Home Grown, a company specializing in design, installation, and maintenance of vegetable and herb gardens, orchards, and vineyards for homeowners. She lives in Pasadena, California, where she is also a cooking instructor, garden writer, wife, and mother of three children.

James Baggett is Emeritus Professor of Horticulture at Oregon State University in Corvallis, Oregon. During his 40-year career at OSU, he was a vegetable breeder, working mainly with green beans, peas, tomatoes, and broccoli. Since his retirement in 1995, he continues to be an enthusiastic gardener.

ILLUSTRATION CREDITS

DAVID CAVAGNARO: cover and pages 1, 6, 10, 30-31, 37, 40, 46 left, 55, 58, 62, 65, 78, 80, 81 bottom, 82 top and bottom, 85, 86 top and bottom, 88, 89, 93, 96, 97, 98, 99, 100, 101
SKIP JOHNS: page 8-9
MONTICELLO MOUNTAIN: page 11
SUZY BALES: 13, 24-25, 26
JUDYWHITE: 15, 16
LOUISA JONES: page 19,
CATHY WILKINSON BARASH: 54 left
RENEE SHEPHERD: 54 right
ALAN DETRICK: page 56
DAVE RUSK: 66
CHRISTINE DOUGLAS: 4, 81 top
DAYNA S. LANE: page 95
DEREK FELL: pages 13, 21, 43, 46 right, 52, 60, 68 right, 69, 70, 71, 73. 102
CARY HAZLEGROVE: pages 47, 48

INDEX

Brooklyn Botanic Garden
21st-Century Gardening Series

For further information please contact the Brooklyn Botanic Garden
1000 Washington Avenue   Brooklyn, New York 11225   (718) 622-4433 ext. 265   www.bbg.org

Watch our garden grow in your very own mailbox!

From Great Neck to Great Bend, Big River to Little Creek, over 20,000 people in all 50 states enjoy the bountiful benefits of membership in the **Brooklyn Botanic Garden** – including our renowned gardening publications.

Brooklyn Botanic Garden Membership

The splendor that makes the Brooklyn Botanic Garden one of the finest in the world can be a regular part of your life. BBG membership brings you subscriptions to some of the liveliest, best-researched, and most practical gardening publications anywhere – including the next entries in our acclaimed 21st-Century Gardening Series (currently published quarterly). BBG publications are written by expert gardeners and horticulturists, and have won prestigious *Quill and Trowel* awards for excellence in garden publishing.

SUBSCRIBER $35

(Library and Institution Rate $60)

* A full year of *21st-Century Gardening Series* handbooks
* A year's subscription to *Plants & Gardens News*
* Offerings of Signature Seeds, handbooks and videos
* Reciprocal privileges at botanical gardens across the country

Plants & Gardens News – practical tips and suggestions from BBG experts.

FAMILY/DUAL $50

All benefits of SUBSCRIBER, plus

* Membership card for free admission for two adult members and their children under 16
* 10% discount at the Terrace Cafe & Garden Gift Shop
* Free parking for four visits
* Discounts on classes, trips and tours

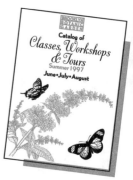

SIGNATURE $125

All benefits of FAMILY, plus

* Your choice of a Signature Plant from our annual catalog of rare and unique shrubs, perennials and house plants
* Unlimited free parking
* A special BBG gift calendar

BBG Catalog – quarterly listing of classes, workshops and tours in the U.S. and abroad, all at a discount.

SPONSOR $300

All benefits of SIGNATURE, plus

* Your choice of <u>two</u> Signature Plants
* Four complimentary one-time guest passes
* Invitations to special receptions

GARDENING BOOKS FOR THE NEXT CENTURY

Brooklyn Botanic Garden's 21st-Century Gardening Series explore frontiers of ecological gardening - offering practical, step-by-step tips on creating environmentally sensitive and beautiful gardens for the 1990s and the new century.

Fall 1997
Please send in this form or contact BBG
for current membership information, higher levels and benefits.

21st-Century Gardening Series – the next handbooks in this acclaimed library.